OUR ORTHODOX HOLY FAMILY:

A JOYFUL JOURNEY WITH JESUS AND MARY

ORTHODOX LOGOS PUBLISHING

OUR ORTHODOX HOLY FAMILY
A JOYFUL JOURNEY WITH JESUS AND MARY

by Deacon David Lochbihler, J.D.

Front Cover photograph by Adrienne L. Meador

Back Cover photograph by Patricia G. Coldewey

Book cover design and interior layout by Max Mendor

Publishers Maxim Hodak & Max Mendor

© 2023, Deacon David Lochbihler, J.D.

© 2023, Orthodox Logos Publishing,

The Netherlands

www.orthodoxlogos.com

ISBN: 978-1-80484-011-5

This book is in copyright. No part of this publication may be reproduced, stored in a retrieval system or transmitted in any form or by any means without the prior permission in writing of the publisher, nor be otherwise circulated in any form of binding or cover other than that in which it is published without a similar condition, including this condition, being imposed on the subsequent purchaser.

DEACON DAVID LOCHBIHLER, J.D.

OUR ORTHODOX HOLY FAMILY:
A JOYFUL JOURNEY WITH JESUS AND MARY

ORTHODOX LOGOS PUBLISHING

CONTENTS

Acknowledgements 9
Prologue – The Joy of Family 13
Chapter One – Jesus and Mary 22
Chapter Two – A Holy Child Speaks 25
Chapter Three – The Joy of the Journey 31
Chapter Four – A Mother in Despair 39
Chapter Five – Earthly Parents 46
Chapter Six – Heavenly Father 50
Chapter Seven – Five Greek Words 58
Chapter Eight – Theory One: Person 68
Chapter Nine – Theory Two: Place 72
Chapter Ten – Theory Three: Thing 80
Chapter Eleven – Theory Four: Ambivalence 87
Chapter Twelve – Theory Five: Integration 93
Chapter Thirteen – Theory Six: Pilgrimage 97
Chapter Fourteen – The Boy Jesus in the Temple . . . 102
Epilogue – Best Friends Forever 109
Bibliography 122
About the Author 127

To
Emily Grace
Olivia Anne
James Patrick
Clare Love
Charlotte Frances
and
Our Favourite Cat Louie

The Mother's sorrow oh so deep!
As the awful truth hit her, she began to weep.
Her darling Son, her Messiah, her Lord!
To everyone His whereabouts she had implored.

Mary and Joseph both searched for their Son.
For two days they saw no sign of Him, not one!
Oh glorious Theotokos, what awful woe!
A parent's peace you did forego.

On the third day they found Him, in the temple He was.
When asked, He said because,
"Did you not know that I must be about My Father's business?"
No need to have searched with such anxiousness.

Olivia Anne Wetzel

ACKNOWLEDGEMENTS

Biblical translations fascinate. Compare these two translations of the first recorded words of Jesus when He visited the Jerusalem Temple at the age of twelve.

"And he said unto them, How is it that ye sought me? wist ye not that I must be about my Father's business" (Luke 2:49 KJV)?

And He said to them, "Why *is it* that you were looking for Me? Did you not know that I had to be in My Father's *house*" (Luke 2:49 NASB)?

Saint Luke nearly two millennia ago writing the original manuscript did not use the Greek words for either "business" or "house" in his Temple narrative. Biblical scholars debated for centuries the precise English words to best express what Jesus originally said in this most memorable verse. Saint Luke chose only these two questions to place in God's Word among the thousands of words spoken by Jesus during the first thirty years of His life.

This book truly embodies a long labour of love. Begun more than fifteen years ago, the birth of this new book springs from a deep joy experienced by enthusiastically exploring and prayerfully pondering five Greek words within one single Biblical verse.

Thank you to Father Patrick and Khouria Kerrie Cardine, Deacon Douglas and Shamassy Phyllis King, and the wonder-full people of Saint Patrick Orthodox Church in Bealeton, Virginia, especially my numerous Pen Pals, for your decade-long love and support. We experience "heaven on earth" each Sunday morning. Lauds and Mass last more than two hours, yet our communal worship seems timeless as if only fifteen minutes pass. A source of abundant joy each Sunday also occurs after Lauds and Mass: playing the baseball card game with Mark Ross, consulting with Craft Captain Luci Marie, comparing manuscripts with fellow author Olivia Anne, discussing literature with Evangeline Sophia, helping Lucas Otar place the priest's vestments for the next Mass, walking outside with Maggie McLaurin, swapping fantasy football teams with Jadon Kai, trading fantasy football players with Knox Hutchins, talking about the Houston Astros with James Patrick, teaching Maximus Ashby to like Notre Dame more than Alabama, playing catch with softball star Natalie Grace, enjoying how much Sola Elise loves her Orthodox school, and receiving a handwritten letter from Millie Ruth, a myriad of amazing adventures following our Sunday Divine Liturgy.

A special thank you to my friend Scott Richardson for meticulously editing my draft manuscript of this book. Scott worked tirelessly to send substantive suggestions and catch typographical errors. Our friendship dates back a decade. After being tonsured as subdeacons, we received certificates from Saint Stephen's Course of Studies and earned Master's degrees from Balamand University. We continue our studies by reading and discussing in depth an array of Orthodox books through our informal yet informative Balamand Book Club get togethers.

I am eternally grateful to Metropolitan Kallistos Ware of blessed memory, Father Peter Gillquist of blessed memory, his beloved wife Khouria Marilyn Gillquist, Father Peter Jon and Khouria Kristina Gillquist, Father Alexander Atty of blessed memory, Father Anthony Messeh, Father Paul Girguis, Father Edward Hughes, Father Thomas Palke, Father Abbot Theodore Phillips, Dom Joseph-Marie, Dame Sophia of blessed memory, Dame Olga of blessed memory, Metropolitan Abbot Jonah Paffhausen, Hieromonk Father Aidan Keller, Father Aurel Sas and his wife Presvytera Lidia of blessed memory, and their son Father Ciprian and his wife Presvytera Maggie Sas for guiding and inspiring me during my wondrous Orthodoxy journey.

Professional and collegial thanks to David and Jo Thoburn, Dean of Students Anthony Pangle, Dean of Operations Angela Etter, Assistant to the Dean of Operations Marcella McAndrews, exceptional fourth-grade colleague Kimberly Dow, and our fantastic fourth-grade scholars at The Fairfax Christian School in Dulles, Virginia.

A heartfelt thank you to my beloved mother as she recently attained an historic lifetime achievement. Mom is still playing cards with superb skill (and winning!) at one hundred years of age, and a deep and abiding love extends to the rest of my family: Fred and his wife Whitney, my nephew Fred and his wife Tania Xiong and their children Frederick Fuechee and Leilana Hli Nra, Doctor Lyn, Vince and his wife Judy, my niece Angela and Kevin and their sons Grant and Nolan, my niece Stephanie and her son Isaac, and my nephew Brett Jordan.

A final, essential thank you to my faithful publisher Maxim Hodak, Esquire, and my excellent editor, Max Mendor. My association with Orthodox Logos in the Netherlands brings great joy to my heart. Your commitment to sharing Orthodox scholarship both deepens our faith and enriches our world.

Every single error in this book is entirely my own. I would love to hear from you, my beloved reader, if any small part of this work touches your heart.

Friends in Jesus and Mary,
Deacon David Lochbihler, J.D.
Saint Patrick Orthodox Church
Tuesday 11 October 2022
Feast of the Motherhood of the Blessed Virgin Mary
orthodoxdeacondavid@gmail.com

PROLOGUE

THE JOY OF FAMILY

Dad lay on his deathbed. The year was 1983.

Having the best Dad in the world makes for the most wonder-full childhood memories. Dad came home after work one day with the greatest gift ever, and it wasn't anyone's birthday. Baseball cards! My first baseball card was a 1966 Topps Willie Mays. Dad also brought home a simple one-dollar baseball card game, and we played season after season with the baseball cards and the card game, keeping stats and enjoying memorable family fun.

Our baseball card games became more advanced as we children grew older. In one strategic game, you could select your own players, and Dad looked back to his own childhood four decades past and played with his favourite team, the 1919 Chicago White Sox. Dad grew up in Chicago and went with the South Siders. For those of you unfamiliar with baseball history, some of Dad's favourite players cavorted with gamblers, threw the 1919 World Series when Dad was nine, and were kicked out of baseball for life. As we played our baseball board games, these disgraced baseball players, the Black Sox, fondly recalled from Dad's early childhood, were the stars of his team.

Dad took my brother Vince and I to our first major league baseball game on Saturday 22 April 1966 at Wrigley

Field in Chicago. When you are nine years old and you first see the beautiful green field and majestic ivy outfield fence after a few years of watching the game on a black-and-white television, you experience a timeless memory to last a lifetime. My brother Vince and I brought our gloves, and as we walked to our seats, we watched in awe and wonder as if entering the most magnificent Gothic Cathedral. All of a sudden, unbeknownst to us, a foul ball came directly towards us. As we stood and stared into space, mitts in hand, we were not aware of the growing fervor around us. I recall seeing the baseball on the ground, Dad reaching for it, but another fan snatching it just ahead of him. Vince and I wore our mitts this ballgame and the next at Wrigley waiting for and expecting another foul ball that would not arrive until a quarter of a century later.

Beginning during my fourth-grade school year, Dad was now sixty years old. Dad and I began hanging out together each Saturday. We would begin our weekend adventure at his office. While Dad worked on his clients' insurance policies, I calculated batting averages for the hitters and earned run averages (with the help of a slide rule) for the pitchers. After a pickup or delivery to Arnold Palmer Dry Cleaners, we headed for the Fort Wayne Public Library. Dad picked up some books to read at home on his favourite chair, and I headed for the sports section to read about the baseball, football, and basketball stars. We then would drive to Northcrest Shopping Center and soon, better yet, to an amazing new thing in America, the indoor mall at Glenbrook. We concluded our fine morning together with a visit to Ponderosa Steak House. Our Saturday adventures continued for about seven years until my junior year in high school, ordinary weekend tasks building precious lifelong childhood memories.

Although our whole family enjoyed vacations together at McCormick's Creek State Park in Indiana, and we all had different favourite teams, I inherited from Dad his love for Chicago sports teams loved from his own childhood. We travelled to Rensselaer, Indiana, a couple summers to watch the Chicago Bears during their summer training camp at Saint Joseph's College. Dad took a memorable picture of me with legendary All-Pro linebacker Dick Butkus, and in my autograph book from 1968, with Dad's help, I secured autographs from many players including running backs Gale Sayers and Brian Piccolo, their biracial friendship featured a few years later in a fantastic family film, *Brian's Song*.

After a few years, I followed my brother Fred's footsteps and enrolled at the University of Notre Dame in Indiana, and Mom and Dad retired to Sun City Center, a golf retirement community, in Florida. During one summer vacation, I remember playing Dad with one of our most skillful baseball board games from my childhood. This particular game required a lot of thought and strategy. As a college student, the game seemed so simple to me, and I crushed Dad by double digits, showing no mercy. Many years later, thinking about my life and the many good times together with Dad, I thought back to our many baseball card and board game seasons together, and something occurred to me. Looking back, it seems like Dad won most all of our regular seasons, but somehow, when it came time for the World Series, I always seemed to win the championship. It dawned on me that Dad most likely let me win the coveted World Series crown at the end of every season we played together. I then recalled how I showed no mercy and ran up the score against Dad when I in college, and I felt quite ashamed.

After Notre Dame, I attended the University of Texas School of Law, and Dad was there for my graduation in Austin, Texas. His visit was memorable. We watched the Texas Longhorns play a college baseball game, and I sat between Dad and my friend Stacey. A booming foul ball touched the sky and was heading straight towards us. Here was another chance to catch a foul ball, this time without a mitt. Unhindered, the ball would have landed on Stacey's head. I reached up, the ball hit my hand, and sadly bounced about ten feet in the air, a fumbled foul ball as the crowd sighed. As I rubbed my hand to get rid of the sting, Stacey asked, "Did you hurt your hand?" Dad quipped, "The only thing he hurt was his pride." During that Texas visit, Dad asked me to drive to a suburban neighborhood, and in one of the houses, Dad met Bib Falk, a famous Texas Longhorn baseball coach for many years. Mr. Falk was Dad's favourite player, a 1920 major league rookie joining the Chicago White Sox a year after the Black Sox Scandal, when Dad was ten. Dad came out of the house with an old autographed photograph of his boyhood hero.

Cancer struck Dad a few years later. Cancer is the most hated and dreadful of diseases. Any family suffering through cancer understands the deep pain of this deadly disease. Yet for one brief moment as Dad suffered, Mom sought a pathway towards hope. Mom had seen a segment on the television news show called 20/20, with a Roman Catholic priest, Father Dennis Kelleher of blessed memory, engaged in a faith healing ministry. A healing Mass was scheduled in Chicago, and Mom and Dad flew into O'Hare Airport with our family gathering to attend Mass with Dad.

I cannot recall ever seeing Dad sick a day in his life, and it was quite jarring to see him quite tired and sickly arriving at O'Hare in a wheelchair. Our family drove to the church. During the healing service, everyone wanting a blessing lined up in the front of the church by the altar rail, and Father Kelleher laid hands on everyone's head and prayed. We all need healing, and we all need prayer. The time seemed to move along somewhat quickly as Father Kelleher prayed and blessed each person. Father Kelleher approached and laid his hands on Dad's head. Unlike anyone else in the church, Dad spent an inordinate amount of time with Father Kelleher. I saw Dad cry for the first time in my life. Father Kelleher continued praying softly and powerfully in Christ as Dad wept. Our family felt something profound was happening.

Dad still suffered with cancer, yet an unexpected blessing for Dad occurred. Despite his widespread cancer and throughout the many months of his debilitating sickness, Dad felt no pain, and this freedom from pain mystified Dad's health care providers. One nurse told us it was inexplicable that despite cancer affecting so much of his body, Dad felt no pain. Although not healed, both the absence of pain and the shedding of tears truly blessed Dad.

A special hospital bed with an oxygen tank was set up in Mom and Dad's Sun City Center living room as Dad's condition continued to deteriorate. By the time I arrived from Illinois to keep watch with Mom, Dad had slipped into a coma. Mom laboured with grace and courage to take care of Dad during this final, deeply sad and silent time. One day, all of a sudden, Dad slipped out of his comatose state and looked around, his eyes darting back and forth, alert and troubled, as if suddenly awakening from a long slumber. Mom and I were both excited to be able to communicate with Dad, and we immediately began talking to him. After a few short minutes, Mom asked Dad, "Do you see David?" Although my face was inches from his, Dad shook his head no. Mom then asked Dad, "Do you see Jesus?" Dad nodded yes. Within seconds Dad slipped back into his coma. The next day, as I said the Rosary, holding Dad's hand, my father suddenly ceased breathing, or so it seemed. About forty-five seconds later, there was a very deep breath. About forty-five seconds later, another very deep breath. One more deep breath, and Dad was gone.

I did not cry then, and I did not cry at Dad's funeral. About one month later, at a youth retreat, I could not stop crying. For about forty-five minutes during the Stations of the Cross, as we sang this most beautiful song "Tell the People," memorized now nearly forty years later, the tears flowed freely:

> "Last night Jesus came to me
> Wiped the tears from my eyes
> He said not to worry,
> He would stay by my side.
>
> "Tell the people I love them,
> Tell the people I care,
> When they feel far away from me,
> Tell the people I'm there."

I simply could not stop crying, an uncontrollable gift of tears.

A few years later, I lived in South Minneapolis, by coincidence three blocks from where George Floyd was murdered during the summer of 2020. I moved to this special neighborhood by church and school three decades ago in

1992. Mom refurnished her Florida home and bought a new recliner. Knowing how much I loved Dad, Mom did want to discard Dad's old recliner without checking with me first. She somehow arranged with a trucking company to ship Dad's brown La-Z-Boy recliner to me all the way from Florida to Minnesota.

I kept the recliner for the past thirty years, moving with it quite often, from Minnesota to South Carolina, from Virginia to Indiana and back. As you can expect, the chair gradually became worn and torn, with frayed and tattered arms and broken reclining gears. At one point about a decade ago, the gears were so broken, the chair could not even be used at all. But a church member skilled in carpentry made the chair usable for a few more years.

Another decade passed, and Dad's old recliner continued deteriorating. Luckily the chair was locked in one somewhat comfortable position. One of the subdeacons at our church excels in household renovations. I offered $100.00 to him to try to fix the gears. I told him about Dad and how the old recliner had great sentimental value for me. Yet realizing a chair half-a-century-old may soon be past repair, I added this caveat: If my friend could not fix Dad's old recliner, I asked Subdeacon James to finally toss it without letting me know. It simply would pass in the night as a fond but distant memory of Dad without me knowing for sure it was gone forever.

Nearly nine months passed and, hearing nothing, I assumed the chair finally was finished for good. After school one day, arriving home, I saw a most unexpected surprise. I was stunned to see what looked like a new recliner. My first thought was that Subdeacon James had somehow found a new recliner for me. Looking more closely, I realized this new chair actually was Dad's old recliner, completely reupholstered with leather and featuring a new gear system!

Subdeacon James almost gave up, and the chair looked like a goner for sure. Yet he persisted, thinking outside the box and asking for assistance as necessary. He knew how much I loved Dad and, how anyone who has lost a parent knows, how I still think about him every day, nearly forty years after holding Dad's hand on his deathbed. The chair was broken, other chairs were more comfortable, but because it reminded me of Dad, the old recliner was priceless, a giver of precious memories.

Subdeacon James discovered a skilled professional in a nearby larger city in Northern Virginia. The chair could be fixed, yet the repair work would be extensive and far more expensive than I anticipated. He brought the matter before our Parish Council at Saint Patrick Orthodox Church and also mentioned the situation to the servers and acolytes in our Sacristy. A collection was taken, and the necessary funds were raised. My Dad's old recliner, with innumerable precious and priceless memories, both joyful and sorrowful, is now as good as new. The gears work superbly, the old, torn leather has been completely refurbished, and the chair is at its best since Dad first sat in it more than two score years ago.

Mom this year turned one hundred, and her thoughtfulness and kindness placed in her mind and heart the unorthodox idea of shipping an old recliner across the country to a son still missing his dad. I call Mom on the telephone each Sunday afternoon after going to church, the same time each week. I knew this story would bring great joy to her heart. When I shared with her about the kind and generous people at Saint Patrick Orthodox Church, and how Dad's old recliner was now as good as new, Mom said, "Tell your friends at church that I really appreciate this. It's a keepsake. Tell them I appreciate it with all my heart."

So blessed to be serving as a Deacon at the finest Orthodox church.

This simple story about an old chair, the joy of childhood memories, and the sorrow of cancer and death, brings the joyful sorrow of family, friendship, and faith forcefully to my heart. Faith and family, life and death. Thoughts about the Holy Family come readily to mind. What does Sacred Scripture teach us about the Birth of Jesus and the Finding of Jesus in the Temple? What does Holy Tradition teach us about the Childhood of the Theotokos and the Death of Saint Joseph?

This book explores one historical event in the life of the Holy Family: The Boy Jesus at the Jerusalem Temple at the age of twelve as described in Luke 2:41-52. Specifically, five Greek words – εν τοις του πατρος μου, the first recorded words of Jesus in Sacred Scripture – are explored in depth. Remarkably "He did nothing while He was a child, save only that one thing to which Luke has testified (Luke ii. 46), that at the age of twelve years He sat hearing the doctors, and was thought admirable for His questioning."[1] The relationship between the Boy Jesus and the Holy Family arising from this magnificent childhood adventure will be the sole focus of this book.

---

[1] Saint Chrysostom, "Homilies on the Gospel of St. John," *A Select Library of the Nicene and Post-Nicene Fathers of the Christian Church*, ed. Philip Schaff, vol. XIV (Edinburgh: T&T Clark, 1989), 74.

CHAPTER ONE

JESUS AND MARY

Jesus and Mary interact in dramatic fashion throughout the four Gospel accounts, each inspired author offering a unique understanding of this most remarkable relationship. Saint Luke's first two chapters present a rare and impressive glimpse into the Annunciation of Mary, Mary's visit to Elizabeth, the birth and purification of the baby Jesus, and Jesus' visit to the Jerusalem temple at the age of twelve. Saint Matthew mentions the circumcision of Jesus and adds the gifts of gold, frankincense, and myrrh from the Magi, the Holy Family's flight into Egypt, and their return to Nazareth. The Synoptic writers include a description of Jesus early in His ministry hearing of His mother and family outside and telling His followers, "For whosoever shall do the will of God, the same is my brother, and my sister, and mother."[2] Saint John the beloved disciple stood at the foot of the Cross and received the Blessed Virgin Mary as his mother.

How do we make Jesus and Mary our best friends? We answer this question by exploring in depth the crux of the conversation between twelve-year-old Jesus and His Mother Mary when she and Joseph found Him in the Jerusalem temple.

---

[2] Mark 3:35 NASB.

The Child continued to grow and become strong, increasing in wisdom; and the grace of God was upon Him. Now His parents went to Jerusalem every year at the Feast of the Passover. And when He became twelve, they went up there according to the custom of the Feast; and as they were returning, after spending the full number of days, the boy Jesus stayed behind in Jerusalem. But His parents were unaware of it, but supposed Him to be in the caravan, and went a day's journey; and they began looking for Him among their relatives and acquaintances. When they did not find Him, they returned to Jerusalem looking for Him. Then, after three days they found Him in the temple, sitting in the midst of the teachers, both listening to them and asking them questions. And all who heard Him were amazed at His understanding and His answers. When they saw Him, they were astonished; and His mother said to Him, "Son, why have You treated us this way? Behold, Your father and I have been anxiously looking for You." And He said to them, "Why is it that you were looking for Me? Did you not know that I had to be in My Father's house?" But they did not understand the statement which He had made to them. And He went down with them and came to Nazareth, and He continued in subjection to them; and His mother treasured all these things in her heart. And Jesus kept increasing in wisdom and stature, and in favor with God and men.[3]

---

[3] Luke 2:40-52 NASB.

The discovery of the Boy Jesus in the Jerusalem temple remains one of the most poignant and wonder-full occurrences in all of Sacred Scripture.

> At that moment a man and a woman came through the colonnade with hurried steps. The man stopped at the edge of the circle, astonished at what he saw. But the woman came into the center and put her arm around the Boy.
> "My boy," she cried, "why hast thou done this to us? See how sorrowful thou hast made me and thy father, looking everywhere for thee?"
> "Mother," he answered, "why did you look everywhere for me with sorrow? Did you not know that I would be in my Father's house? Must I not begin to think of the things my Father wants me to do?"
> Thus the lost Boy was found again, and went home with his parents to Nazareth. The old rabbi blessed him as he left the Temple.
> But had he really been lost, or was he finding his way?[4]

This book will explore five Greek words – εν τοις του πατρος μου – contained within the first recorded words of Jesus in Luke 2:49. Our understanding of these five words will create an avenue in our hearts to deepen our loving and intimate relationship with our best friends Jesus and Mary. Five Greek words – εν τοις του πατρος μου – let the journey begin.

---

[4] Henry van Dyke, *The Lost Boy* (New York: Harper, 1914), 68-69.

CHAPTER TWO

A HOLY CHILD SPEAKS

To begin our journey, we must walk in the footprints of Boy Jesus.

> My heart leaps up when I behold
>   A rainbow in the sky:
> So was it when my life began;
> So is it now I am a man;
> So be it when I shall grow old,
>   Or let me die!
> The Child is father of the Man;
> And I could wish my days to be
> Bound each to each by natural piety.[5]

With these words, William Wordsworth inadvertently offers a glimpse into the significant interplay between the Boy Jesus and the adult He will become. "The poet Wordsworth says that the child is father of the man; and surely in these words of Jesus we get a hint of all that the man Jesus is ever to become."[6] Jesus' first recorded words at the age of twelve

---

[5] William Wordsworth, "My Heart Leaps Up When I Behold," *Selected Poems of William Wordsworth*, ed. Solomon Francis Gingerich (Boston: Houghton Mifflin, 1923), 66.

[6] James Hastings, ed., *The Great Texts of the Bible: St. Luke* (Grand

portend His future Messianic mission, and it is relevant He speaks these words to His Mother in the form of two questions.

Writing under the inspiration of the Holy Spirit, Saint Luke describes the temple scene from Jesus' childhood with both vivid detail and engaging dialogue. How did the evangelist learn about this amazing conversation between the Boy Jesus and His Mother? The Virgin Mary experienced an array of divinely memorable events from the childhood of Jesus, "and His mother treasured all these things in her heart."[7] Finally finding the Boy Jesus in the temple must have been one of her most treasured memories. "All this temple-scene, as Calvin says, would have faded before long from the memories of men, had not Mary laid it all up in her heart, to bring it out long afterwards, along with other treasures of the same kind, for the enriching of all men who would afterwards read her marvelous story."[8] The temple scene is so graphically illustrated, it is as if Mary herself recalled the event and shared it with the evangelist many years after Jesus died and rose from the dead, allowing Saint Luke to write his gospel account as if he were an eyewitness. "Observing the prominence that is given to the parents, and how the story enlarges upon what they thought and felt, we shall not have much doubt in accepting the hypothesis that it was none other than Mary from whom Luke received such intimate details."[9]

Rapids, MI: Baker, 1976), 10:127.

[7] Luke 2:51b NASB.

[8] Alexander Whyte, *The Walk, Conversation and Character of Jesus Christ our Lord* (Edinburgh: Oliphant, Anderson & Ferrier, 1905), 51.

[9] Alexander Maclaren, *After the Resurrection* (New York: Funk & Wagnalls, n.d.), 193.

"The pen of inspiration has recorded the incident as shedding a most beautiful light on the character and history of the sacred child."[10] Upon considering all the events in the first three decades of Jesus' life on earth as both a child and a young man, Saint Luke records only this one. As to His character, the Boy Jesus spoke openly and honestly before the learned temple doctors, as both an active listener and an avid interrogator: "Then, after three days they found Him in the temple, sitting in the midst of the teachers, both listening to them and asking them questions."[11] By this intriguing dialogue, Jesus distinguished Himself before His scholarly listeners with astute wisdom: "And all who heard Him were amazed at His understanding and His answers."[12] By recording this most significant incident and bringing Jesus' childhood into the light, Saint Luke offers his readers a penetrating glance into Jesus' ultimate uniqueness.

The lack of any specific information about any other incident from Jesus' childhood and early life makes this pericope, this most exceptional Biblical passage, even more fascinating. "A veil of silence has fallen on so much of the pre-natal facts. His boyhood, and His adolescent years, that it is a relief for us to find this one solitary story from His boyhood."[13] With thirty years of words and deeds to consider, the inspired evangelist focuses on only two questions asked by the Boy Jesus while speaking with His Mother Mary in the Jerusalem temple. "In thirty years, one saying,

---

[10] A. C. Kendrick, *The Moral Conflict of Humanity and Other Papers* (Philadelphia: American Baptist PS, 1894), 137.

[11] Luke 2:46 NASB.

[12] Ibid., Luke 2:47.

[13] David E. Anderson, *Gospel Firsts: Messages on the First Things in the Bible* (N.p.: Anderson, 1947), 41.

and only one, survives. These are the first recorded words of Jesus, and every syllable is precious."[14] These dynamic words of the Boy offer a glimpse into the Man.

"The forty-ninth verse of the second chapter of Luke's Gospel should be printed in letters of gold a finger deep. For that absolutely priceless verse has preserved to us the very first words that ever fell from the youthful lips of our Lord."[15] More accurately, Saint Luke presents the first recorded words of Jesus in the form of two most memorable questions. This premier saying of Jesus continues to be a source of significant exegetical enthusiasm among scholars and theologians of all faiths. "But there is a class of men among us who are enabled and enjoined to give all their time and all their thoughts to nothing else but to such inquiries as these. I refer to that elect, and honourable, and enviable class of men that we call student of New Testament exegesis. Surely they are the happiest and the most enviable of all men, who have been set apart to nothing else but to the understanding and the opening up of the hid treasures of God's Word and God's Son."[16]

Numerous Biblical scholars for several centuries have struggled to make sense of the five Greek words – εν τοις του πατρος μου – from Luke 2:49. What they reveal is the lack of any definitive answer to the dilemma posed by this short phrase. After Mary and Joseph find Him in the temple, the Boy Jesus begins his second question to His Mother with the phrase, "Did you not know that I must be..."[17] What

---

[14] Hastings, *The Great Texts of the Bible: St. Luke*, 127.

[15] Whyte, *The Walk, Conversation and Character of Jesus Christ our Lord*, 59.

[16] Ibid., 53.

[17] Luke 2:49b NASB.

Jesus next says leads to some confusion. A typical scholarly analysis follows:

> 'I must be about the affairs of my Father'. There has been controversy over the meaning of these words for centuries. The two interpretations which have received most support are 'I must be in the house of my Father' and 'I must be about the affairs of my Father'; as a variant of the second version, one also finds 'I must be *engaged* in my Father's business'. Divers other explanations have been given.[18]

The five Greek words – εν τοις του πατρος μου – may be narrowed down to only two. "The words of the Christ Boy, Luke 2, 49, contain an obscure expression, *en tois*, which is truly a crux interpretum."[19] These two little words, one a preposition, the other a definite article, have confounded Biblical scholars for hundreds of years. "Scholars and exegetes have battled over it, and expanded erudition to a vast amount, especially during the last three centuries, and the only result has been a great diversity of opinion."[20]

Different Bible translations exacerbate the problem inherent in presenting a precise articulation of Jesus' words in Luke 2:49. For example, although the New American Standard Bible and the New King James Version present a slight variation from Jesus' first question to His Mother, the second question is presented in two significantly dif-

---

[18] Henk J. de Jonge, "Sonship, Wisdom, Infancy: Luke ii. 41-51a," *New Testament Studies* 24 (1978): 333.

[19] Patrick J. Temple, "What is to be understood by *En Tois* Luke 2, 49?" *The Irish Theological Quarterly* 17 (1922): 248.

[20] Ibid.

ferent ways. Whereas the New American Standard Bible states, "Did you not know that I had to be in my Father's house?"[21], the New King James Version says, "Did you not know that I must be about My Father's business?"[22] Five Greek words – εν τοις του πατρος μου – lie at the heart of these translation differences. Our exploration of the Boy Jesus' use of this phrase while speaking with His Mother will deepen our mutual love for the Holy Child and the Virgin Mary.

---

[21] Luke 2:49b NASB.

[22] Luke 2:49b NKJV.

CHAPTER THREE

THE JOY OF THE JOURNEY

THE world is charged with the grandeur of God.
  It will flame out, like shining from shook foil;
  It gathers to a greatness, like the ooze of oil
Crushed. Why do men then now not reck his rod?
Generations have trod, have trod, have trod;
  And all is seared with trade; bleared, smeared with toil;
  And wears man's smudge and shares men's smell: the soil
Is bare now, nor can foot feel, being shod.

And for all this, nature is never spent;
  There lives the dearest freshness deep down things;
And though the last lights off the black West went
  Oh, morning, at the brown brink eastward, springs—
Because the Holy Ghost over the bent
  World broods with warm breast and with ah! bright
      wings.[23]

Gerard Manley Hopkins beautifully describes the wonder of God's creation. God's grandeur charges the world; the dearest freshness lies deep down inside; the Holy Ghost

---

[23] Gerard Manley Hopkins, "God's Grandeur," *Poems of Gerard Manley Hopkins*, 3rd ed., edited by W. H. Gardner (New York & London: Oxford University Press, 1948), 70.

inspires. These vivid images paint a magnificent picture, one the Holy Family would have appreciated with reverence as they travelled from Nazareth to Jerusalem for Passover. The journey would have been a fascinating one for the young boy. "He had come up to Jerusalem and the Temple with the innocent and ingenuous expectancy of youth."[24] Like any other child of twelve, the sheer anticipation of the Passover trip would have been a source of joy in and of itself, and it is easy to imagine His Mother Mary smiling at the enthusiasm of her holy and happy Son.

> The Boy was the joy of the journey. His keen interest in all things seen and heard was like a refreshing spring of water to the older pilgrims, who had so often traveled the same road that they had forgotten that it might be new every morning. His unwearying vigor and pure gladness as he leaped down the hillsides, or scrambled among the rocks far above the path, or roamed through the fields filling his hands with flowers, was like a merry song that cheered the long miles of the way. He was glad to be alive, and it made the others glad to look at him.[25]

This journey comes at a pivotal point in Jesus' young life, between His twelfth and thirteenth birthdays. "The age of religious maturity was, and is, between the ages of twelve and thirteen. It was thought that boys reached puberty at thirteen. Therefore, at twelve, Jesus could well have been

---

[24] Alfred E. Garvie, *Studies in the Inner Life of Jesus* (New York: Hodder & Stoughton, 1907), 110.

[25] Dyke, *The Lost Boy*, 4.

considered as having become 'bar mitzvah' ('son of the Law'), subject to the whole of the Law."[26]

At the age of twelve, Jesus stood on the brink of Jewish manhood. Within less than a year, He and not His parents would be responsible fully for His own actions. Jesus may have imagined the effects of His thirteenth birthday:

> On the morning of this day he put on for the first time the two phylacteries which every Jew wore when he prayed, one on the head, and the other on the left arm. These phylacteries were small square boxes made of parchment, which were attached to the arm and the forehead by long slender straps; in each box there were four tiny cells; and in each cell there was put a strip of vellum on which was written a passage from the books of Exodus and Deuteronomy.[27]

This Passover visit to the Jerusalem temple would have taken several days to complete. Eventually those leading the caravan would shout back the welcome news: Jerusalem, the holy city, is seen! "It was the thrill of a lifetime when the group topped the Mount of Olives and looked across the valley to the holy city nestled on the side of the hill with the dome of the temple rising above the other structures. The dream of several years for this lad was about to be realized."[28] The Boy Jesus undoubtedly listened to the Virgin Mary's stories about the holy city in the course of

---

[26] Lucien Deiss, *Joseph, Mary, Jesus*, trans. Madeleine Beaumont (Collegeville, MN: Liturgical Press, 1996), 109.

[27] Hastings, *The Great Texts of the Bible: St. Luke*, 109.

[28] C. E. Colton, *Expository Studies in the Life of Christ* (Grand Rapids, MI: Zondervan, 1957), 63.

His being taught at home. He undoubtedly learned at His synagogue. He longed for this journey in joyful anticipation for months, perhaps even years. "Now his dream had come true."[29] How did this pivotal event touch Jesus' young and impressionable heart?

> What an evening that was for the Boy! His first sight of the holy city, the city of the great king, the city lifted up and exalted on the sides of the north, beautiful for situation, the joy of the whole earth! He had dreamed of her glory as he listened at his mother's knee to the wonder-tales of David and Solomon and the brave adventures of the fighting Maccabees. He had prayed for the peace of Jerusalem every night as he kneeled by his bed and lifted his young hands toward the holy place. He had tried a thousand times to picture her strength and her splendor, her marvels and mysteries, her multitude of houses and her vast bulwarks, as he strayed among the humble cottages of Nazareth or sat in the low doorway of his own home.[30]

From Jesus' synagogue studies of Sacred Scripture, Jerusalem and her temple would hold a special place in His young heart. "To Him Jerusalem as God's chosen city would be very dear; to Him the Temple as God's abode would seem the most blessed spot on earth; to Him the priests and scribes and all who had any share in the Temple worship, or waited on its ordinances, would seem highly favoured."[31]

---

[29] Dyke, *The Lost Boy*, 14.

[30] Ibid., 13-14.

[31] Garvie, *Studies in the Inner Life of Jesus*, 110.

Arriving from small-town Nazareth, the Boy Jesus eagerly anticipated both the exciting journey to Jerusalem and the intellectual insights offered by the temple priests and scribes.

The magnificence of Jerusalem and the historical and spiritual significance of the Jewish temple would not be lost on the Boy Jesus. "He had come from Nazareth's quiet valley, from association with minds proverbially low, to the great capitol of his country, to view the living monuments of his people's pride and glory, and to feel the attrition of the most cultivated Jewish minds."[32] The Boy Jesus truly would appreciate his visit "to the heart and centre of all the glorious history and appointments of the ancient Scriptures."[33]

Upon arriving in Jerusalem, the Boy Jesus would seek to become acquainted with the Jewish religious leaders within the holy temple confines. "Jesus loved God above all things with all His heart. His interest in the Word of God was so great that when He reached Jerusalem, He was so eager to learn that He lost Himself among the doctors of the Temple."[34] As the Boy Jesus grew in Nazareth, He undoubtedly received much sound spiritual guidance from Mary and Joseph at home. The early events described in the first two chapters of Saint Luke's Gospel certainly were discussed and pondered. Though inspiring, however, the dynamic discourse of His earthly mother and father may have lacked at times the theological depths offered by the temple teachers formally trained in the Jewish law. "In all probability,

---

[32] Joseph A. Seiss, *Lectures on the Gospels*, 4th ed. (Philadelphia: General Council PH, 1908), 199.

[33] Ibid.

[34] Dallas C. Baer, *The Old Gospel for the New Times*, vol. 1 (Burlington, VT: Lutheran Literary Board, 1936), 67.

He had often asked questions that Mary would not answer, and now that He was face to face with the great religious leaders of the nation, He was so eager to ask questions that He forgot everything else, but His Father's business."[35] Well-versed in Sacred Scriptures, Jesus' immersion in the Biblical exegesis from the temple teachers about the Word of God undoubtedly interested and intrigued Him.

"Where a man feels at home tells plainly the story of his life. Jesus when visiting the capital city of His nation forgot everything else and sought the house of worship."[36] Although the visit to the big city in Jerusalem would present an array of sights and sounds to interest a small-town sojourner from Nazareth, the temple best represented the most likely place to worship God. "I picture to my mind how that blessed child loved the place *where his Father was worshipped*."[37] Drawn by His Father's intimate call upon His heart, the Boy Jesus naturally sought this most historical and precious site where the Jewish faithful gathered to worship His Father.

Imagine the Boy Jesus running ahead of the caravan of pilgrims, the first of His fellow travelers to step foot into Jerusalem. This caravan would have been one of thousands ascending the hills surrounding Jerusalem to celebrate the Passover Feast. "One historian estimates that there were 2,700,200 people in Jerusalem to worship, not counting foreigners and those unclean persons not granted the privilege

---

[35] Ibid.

[36] Ibid., 68.

[37] C. H. Spurgeon, *C.H. Spurgeon's Sermons on Crises in the Life of Jesus*, ed. Charles T. Cook, vol. 24 (London: Marshall, 1966), 23 (emphasis in original).

of worshipping in the Temple."[38] At the age of twelve, about to enter into His Jewish manhood, the Boy Jesus would seek to deepen His ever-emerging intimacy with God His Father. "From all of this holiday multitude Jesus stole away to the quiet Temple. He was already beginning to realize His divine mission and felt that He had to be about His Father's business."[39]

The Gospel accounts do not directly address either the Boy Jesus' conscious thoughts or His subconscious state of mind during this historic visit to the Jerusalem temple. "The temple was the most natural place for Jesus to be in, for whether He was conscious or not of His relation to His Father's house, there must have been in His subconsciousness, at least, a strong attraction toward and for the building which had its only interpretation in Him."[40] As a child of twelve, the Boy Jesus undoubtedly entered the temple with a sense of awe and wonder. "Unconscious of the true reasons for His close affinity for the temple, Jesus must have loved and venerated the building which incarnated and preserved all the traditions of His people and of God's grace and providence."[41] Jesus came to worship and learn. "He was in the Temple, not as a critic, still less as a cynic, but as a worshipper and an inquirer."[42] The temple brought great joy to His young heart. "He looked upon the Temple as being for the time the residence of God, where he manifested himself in an unusual degree, and so this

---

[38] Baer, *The Old Gospel for the New Times*, 68.

[39] Ibid.

[40] George F. Pentecost, *The Birth and Boyhood of Jesus* (New York: ATS, 1897), 339-340.

[41] Ibid., 341.

[42] Garvie, *Studies in the Inner Life of Jesus*, 111.

holy child looked upon those walls and courts with delight as his Father's house."[43] The Boy Jesus inevitably found Himself at home in the temple.

---

[43] Spurgeon, *C.H. Spurgeon's Sermons on Crises in the Life of Jesus*, 13-14.

CHAPTER FOUR

A MOTHER IN DESPAIR

In Egypt and in poverty, I think I see thee, Mary
All glad at heart, all radiant, with joy beyond compare.
What matters exile unto thee? Thy true home cannot vary.
   Hast thou not Jesus with thee still? and with Him
      Heaven is there.
But, oh! in fair Jerusalem, a sorrow, vast, unbounded,
   Indeed o'erwhelmed thy mother-heart with grief beyond
      compare;—
For three days Jesus hid Himself; no word to thee was spoken.
   Thou truly wast an exile then, and knew what exiles
      bear.[44]

With the Passover Feast ending, Mary and Joseph, like thousands of other families traveling by caravan, left the holy city to return home. "After fulfilling the obligations of the Passover celebration which lasted two days, though the whole celebration lasted a week, the family started their journey back to Nazareth."[45] Although "the boy Jesus stayed behind in Jerusalem," Mary and Joseph "were unaware of

---

[44] Sister Teresa of Lisieux, "Why I Love Thee Mary," *The Petals of a "Little Flower"*, trans. Susan L. Emery (Boston: Angel Guardian Press, 1907), 67.

[45] Colton, *Expository Studies in the Life of Christ*, 63.

it, but supposed Him to be in the caravan and went a day's journey; and they began looking for Him among their relatives and acquaintances. When they did not find Him, they returned to Jerusalem looking for Him."[46]

Although we do not know the precise circumstances leading to the Boy Jesus' being left behind, several logical possibilities emerge. According to English monk and scholar Saint Bede the Venerable:

> Someone may ask how could the Son of God, cherished with such care by the Virgin and Joseph, be forgotten and left behind? To which we answer, that it was the custom of the children of Israel that when they were either going or coming from Jerusalem, at the time of the festival, that men and women journeyed separately. Infants and children could go with one or the other parent. Hence, both the Virgin and Joseph thought Jesus was with the other.[47]

Stated another way:

> There were a number of relatives and friends in the traveling party or caravan. Each parent thought that Jesus was in another part of the caravan, but when camp was established for the night, it was obvious that the child was not present. In such a large traveling party it is not difficult to see how the absence of the child would go unnoticed throughout the day.[48]

---

[46] Luke 2:43b-45 NASB.

[47] *The Life of the Virgin, the Theotokos* (Buena Vista, CA: Holy Apostles Convent, 1989), 316-317.

[48] Colton, *Expository Studies in the Life of Christ*, 63.

It also is easy to imagine, in such a large traveling caravan, that many of the men would walk together while many of the women congregated among themselves for the long journey home. The Boy Jesus was twelve years old, nearing Jewish manhood. The Virgin Mary may have thought He would be with Joseph and the men, while Joseph believed the Holy Child walked with His mother.

At some point in time, the stark reality of Jesus' absence inevitably surprised and startled Mary and Joseph to the depth of their being. The caravan traveled from dusk to dawn and pitched their tents one day's journey from Jerusalem. "A bedtime check revealed the startling news that the child Jesus was not in the party."[49] This unfortunate circumstance undoubtedly engendered deep anxiety and consternation in the hearts of Mary and Joseph, with the possibility of an emerging despair developing. "With grave concern and anxiety the mother and father went back to Jerusalem to find the child."[50]

Saint Luke mentions three days as the duration of separation between Jesus and His parents. Part of this time most likely involved travel from and to Jerusalem. Surprisingly, the temple seems to be their final destination. "To be three whole days, searching the whole city up and down sorrowing, and never once to think of going to the temple — it quite baffles me to think what the parents of the child could have had in their thoughts all those three sorrowing days. It is a mystery to me, the more I think of it."[51] Indeed, Mary and Joseph simply may not have no-

---

[49] Ibid.

[50] Ibid.

[51] Whyte, *The Walk, Conversation and Character of Jesus Christ our Lord*, 52.

ticed the Boy Jesus' deep heartfelt yearning to be both in His Father's house and about His heavenly Father's affairs. "Apparently during their seven days' stay they had not taken note of the deep fascination that the sacred precincts had for him."[52]

The night before the Boy Jesus was found in the temple, both Holy Child and His Holy Family laid their heads down to sleep, or to try to sleep, albeit in different locations. Jesus may have thought about the many unanswered questions He hoped to ask the learned doctors and scribes at the beloved temple in the morning. Mary and Joseph probably experienced a deep and fearful insomnia, nearing despair yet placing their trust in God. They may have sought the solace and encouragement of Sacred Scripture, recalling from memory this powerful verse from the prophet Isaiah, "The people that walked in darkness have seen a great light: they that dwell in the land of the shadow of death, upon them hath the light shined."[53] Perhaps they anticipated the words of the seventeenth-century English theologian and historian Thomas Fuller, "It is always darkest just before the day dawneth."[54] Mother and father undoubtedly prayed during a fitful night of fretful sleep for a more successful search in the morning.

The Boy Jesus would remember His first extended visit to the temple for the rest of His life.

....

[52] George A. Barton, *Jesus of Nazareth* (New York: Macmillan, 1932), 96.

[53] Isaiah 9:2 KJV.

[54] Bible or Not, "It is Always Darkest Before the Dawn," accessed October 4, 2010, http://bibleornot.org/its-it-is-always-darkest-before-the-dawn/.

The Boy turned into the long, cool cloisters, with their lofty marble columns and carved roofs of wood, which ran around the inside of the walls. Here he found many groups of people, walking in the broad aisles between the pillars, or seated in the alcoves of Solomon's Porch around the teachers who were instructing them. From one to another of these open schools he wandered, listening eagerly to the different rabbis and doctors of the law.[55]

The youth's decision to remain behind in the temple seems to be the most natural course of action. "After the people had all gone back to their homes, He, remaining behind, would naturally stay in the temple, and, with His awakening mind, seek out the doctors and instructors in the law; and we can well believe that such a Child as Jesus would be warmly welcomed by these wise men."[56] The effect of this visit upon the temple teachers must have been most memorable for them. "How these men were charmed and astonished at the glorious and noble-hearted boy. There he sat in the radiant beauty of innocent childhood."[57] As the Boy Jesus begins His historical dialogue with the learned doctors, the lively interplay of ideas inevitably touched something deep within Jesus' heart, making Him reluctant to leave. "So absorbed was he in exploring the wisdom of the doctors in the Temple and in meditating there, that,

---

[55] Dyke, *The Lost Boy*, 56.

[56] Pentecost, *The Birth and Boyhood of Jesus*, 339.

[57] William Warren Landrum, "Consecrated Childhood," *The American Baptist Pulpit at the Beginning of the Twentieth Century*, ed. Henry Thompson Louthan (Williamsburg, VA: n.n., 1903), 216.

when the caravan of pilgrims started again for Galilee, he remained behind in the Temple."[58]

Luke describes the Boy Jesus as "sitting in the midst of the teachers, both listening to them and asking them questions."[59] What happened in the heart and mind of Jesus? "He was, in fact, a twelve-year-old boy, at the age of adulthood in Jewish eyes, talking with the teachers about what would be his life's work."[60] The Boy Jesus expressed a youthful desire to learn. Besides listening eagerly to the doctors, He probed His audience with precise and piercing questions. "Therefore he allowed the teachers and priests to teach and instruct, but for his own part he asked questions eloquently and listened intelligently and responded thoughtfully. That is also why they were all amazed by his understanding and wisdom, for he was truly amazing."[61]

Jesus' concise answers and probing questions captured the attention of His listeners. "We cannot be wrong in thinking that the startling effect of His words would be due, not to any display of precocious learning, but to the simplicity and directness of His questions and answers."[62] In addition, His young heart, open to learning, filled with wonder and enthusiasm as He and the doctors delved deeply into the Sacred Scriptures. "New subjects were thrown in upon his human intellect. A new world opened to his soul and seized upon his heart, already in holy and peaceful har-

---

[58] Barton, *Jesus of Nazareth*, 96.

[59] Luke 2:46b NASB.

[60] Karen Chakoian, "Luke 2:41-52," *Interpretation* 52 (1998): 190.

[61] Maximus the Confessor, *The Life of the Virgin*, trans. Stephen J. Shoemaker (New Haven and London: Yale University Press, 2012), 88.

[62] Hastings, *The Great Texts of the Bible: St. Luke*, 109.

mony with the deepest underlying Spirit of all."[63] Perhaps a heart already on fire with divine love for His heavenly Father reached new intellectual and emotional depths of intimacy and communion.

Mary and Joseph continued their frantic search for their Son in the highways and the byways of the capital city. Relieved beyond measure, they eventually discover the Boy Jesus in the temple. "Then, after three days they found Him in the temple, sitting in the midst of the teachers, both listening to them and asking them questions."[64] Although this reunion occurs in God's house, Mary and Joseph consider the matter from a more worldly perspective. In this interaction with His human parents, Jesus clearly elucidates His uniquely divine relationship with His heavenly Father, yet Mary and Joseph cannot understand.

---

[63] Seiss, *Lectures on the Gospels*, 199.

[64] Luke 2:46 NASB.

CHAPTER FIVE

EARTHLY PARENTS

> And when, at last, thine eyes again were thy Son's face beholding,
> And love entranced thee, watching Him among the doctors wise,
> "My Child!" thou saidst, "now tell me why thy didst leave my arms enfolding?
> Didst Thou not know we sought for Thee with tear-endimnèd eyes?"
> The Child-God answered to thee then, to thy sweet, patient wooing,
> O Mother whom He loved so well, whose heart was well-nigh broken!
> "How is it that you sought for Me? Wist not I must be doing My Father's work?" Oh, who shall sound the depths those words betoken?[65]

The Blessed Virgin Mary and her husband Joseph approached their Son. "When they saw Him, they were astonished; and His mother said to Him, 'Son, why have You treated us this way? Behold, Your father and I have been

---

[65] Sister Teresa of Lisieux, "Why I Love Thee Mary," 68.

anxiously looking for You.' "[66] Mary spoke to her beloved Son from the deepest recesses of her heart:

> Her words are the spontaneous cry of a mother's heart; let us not subject them to cold analysis. What else would a mother say at a time like this? Whether they are a loving complaint or an affectionate rebuke, Mary's words spring, above all from a desire to know the motive prompting this conduct, so much at variance with the habits of a Son who had been so completely respectful and submissive, and always so anxious to avoid causing them the slightest displeasure.[67]

The Boy Jesus answers His Mother's question with two inquiries of His own, the very first recorded words of Jesus in the Gospels. "And He said to them, 'Why is it that you were looking for Me? Did you not know that I had to be in my Father's house?' "[68] Saint Luke quickly asserts in the very next verse, "But they did not understand the statement which He had made to them."[69] Like many of the mysteries presented in the time before and after Jesus' birth and early years, the Virgin Mary could not fully comprehend the importance of the Boy Jesus' two questions. Mary focuses on the earthly separation and reunion between mother and Son; Jesus speaks of a familial divine relationship beyond the human realm. Because "his words had a mysterious mean-

....

[66] Luke 2:48 NASB.

[67] Ferdinand Prat, *Jesus Christ: His Life, His Teaching, and His Work*, trans. John J. Heenan, vol. 1 (Milwaukee, WI: Bruce, 1950), 123.

[68] Luke 2:49 NASB.

[69] Ibid., Luke 2:50.

ing, whose depths his parents did not at the time reach,"[70] Mary and Joseph failed to understand and could not adequately answer the questions posed by Jesus. At best, "His mother treasured all these things in her heart."[71] Despite Jesus' miraculous conception and astonishing birth and the prophetic words of the prophet Simeon and the prophetess Anna in the temple, Mary could not grasp fully the depths of her twelve-year-old Son's two questions.

Jesus' respectful response placed His earthly parents within a confusing quandary suffused with profound and everlasting divine implications. These spiritual truths would be made manifest in time. "Only the actual playing out of the life of Jesus will eventually make clear all these factors which have come upon Mary and Joseph so suddenly in these two chapters; at the moment, they are overwhelmed as they try to put all the pieces together."[72] Just as Jesus' divine nature and mission undoubtedly perplexed Mary and Joseph, many of the Jews witnessing Jesus' miracles and hearing Him teach failed to comprehend the full significance of these extraordinary events. "This incomprehension is deliberately reported by Luke, for it, like so many other elements of the Infancy Narratives, reflects a future element of the adult life of Jesus and prepares the reader for it – here is foreshadowed the confusion about the identity of the adult Jesus."[73] Faced with two perplexing questions from their Divine Son, Mary and Joseph fail to understand, a result hardly surprising.

---

[70] Prat, *Jesus Christ: His Life, His Teaching, and His Work*, 124.

[71] Luke 2:51b NASB.

[72] John J. Kilgallen, "Luke 2, 41-50: Foreshadowing of Jesus, Teacher," *Biblica* 66 (1985): 559.

[73] Ibid.

Although Mary asks about an earthly father, the Boy Jesus intimately understands His heavenly Father and seeks to express the significance of this divine relationship. "Luke has consciously arranged a sharp contrast by placing so close together Mary's phrasing 'your *father* and I' (*ho patēr sou* – v. 48) and Jesus's phrasing 'in the house of *my Father*' (*tou patros mou* – v. 49)."[74] In talking about her husband Joseph, Mary interprets her Son's appearance in the temple as an ordinary event in her family's life. In shifting the conversation from His earthly to His heavenly Father, Jesus emphasizes His divine rather than earthly origins.

His shift from the temporal to the eternal may be placed in Saint Luke's Gospel to emphasize a significant internal shift within the Boy Jesus' emerging self-awareness. "If we now look more closely at His own words, 'How is it that ye sought Me? Wist ye not that I must be in My Father's house?' (Luke ii. 49), we may learn with some probability the characteristics of His consciousness."[75] Determining the Boy Jesus' inner consciousness may not be accomplished with any degree of precision, but it is possible "that this visit of the young Saviour to the holy city and temple was the means of an enlarged and astonishing spiritual awakening to him."[76] The first recorded words of Jesus, while not providing a definitive analysis of the Holy Child's state of mind, nevertheless may lead to some relevant insights.

---

[74] Ibid., 557 (emphasis in original).
[75] Garvie, *Studies in the Inner Life of Jesus*, 109.
[76] Seiss, *Lectures on the Gospels*, 109.

CHAPTER SIX

HEAVENLY FATHER

> Most high,
> glorious God,
> enlighten the darkness of my heart
> and give me, Lord,
> a correct faith,
> a certain hope,
> a perfect charity,
> sense and knowledge,
> so that I may carry out Your holy and true command.[77]

Jesus' first remarkable words to Mary and Joseph express both a unique understanding of His heavenly Father and a clear sense of mission. Biblical scholars sometimes speculate on the emerging consciousness of the Boy Jesus by focusing on the words and actions occurring in this temple scene eloquently described by Saint Luke. "But this episode is of cardinal importance as shewing the ascendancy which at a particular crisis in adolescence the conception of God as Father has attained over his consciousness."[78] The Boy Jesus'

---

[77] Saint Francis of Assisi, "Prayer Before the Crucifix," *Francis and Clare: The Complete Works*, trans. Regis J. Armstrong and Ignatius C. Brady (New York: Paulist Press, 1982), 103.

[78] William Manson, "The Gospel of Luke," *The Moffat New Testa-*

precise language in Luke 2:49, phrase by phrase, expresses His unique relationship with God the Father.

In response to the question and declaration of the Virgin Mary, Jesus Himself poses two questions. He first asks, "Why is it that you were looking for me?"[79] This initial question may be broken down into its distinctive words and phrases. "Why is it that…" literally means, " 'How is it that?' "[80] Jesus addresses both Mary and Joseph, leading to several interpretations of why this is so. "The 'you' is plural, and so Jesus is answering not only his mother's question but also both parents' amazement and worry."[81] In addition, one may theorize Jesus answers Mary's reproach in verse 48 with a reproach of His own in verse 49. "Answering Mary and Joseph in the plural tones down the reply to Mary's reproach. Indeed, Jesus' own question has something of a reproach in it too."[82] Perhaps the tone of Jesus' first question involves more disappointment than reproach. "The tone of his question is more one of grief that his parents have known him so poorly."[83] Finally, "looking for me" indicates Saint Luke's emphasis of Jesus as the central focus on these questions. "The 'me' in this question and the 'I' in the next question are in the emphatic position in Greek, coming at the very end of both questions."[84]

---

ment Commentary (New York: Hodder & Stoughton, 1963), 23.

[79] Luke 2:49a NASB.

[80] Raymond E. Brown, *The Birth of the Messiah* (New York: Doubleday, 1993), 475.

[81] Ibid.

[82] Joseph A. Fitzmyer, "The Gospel According to Luke (I-IX)," *The Anchor Bible* (Garden City, NY: Doubleday, 1981), 443.

[83] Brown, *The Birth of the Messiah*, 490.

[84] Ibid., 475.

Jesus' first question is subject to varying interpretations. Similarly, His second question has stumped scholars for centuries. "Did you not know that I had to be in My Father's house?"[85] The earliest English translations used the word "wist" to begin this question. "The use of the word 'wist' is an old English word which means 'to know.' It comes from the Saxon 'wissen', from the word knowledge. In the text it is in the past tense, meaning, 'Did you not know?' "[86] The next phrase indicates "that (Jesus) had to be" in His Father's house. Literally from the Greek, this phrase means " 'that… it was necessary (for) me to be.' "[87] These words demonstrate an inner necessity to act.

The Greek word δει, translated as "had to be" or "must," leads to several divergent interpretations regarding Jesus' unique mission. " 'I must be about my Father's business,' or, if we take the R.V., 'in my Father's house'; it comes to nearly the same thing. 'I must be.' He is not His own. He belongs to His Father. He owes to Him His life and its powers."[88]

"The words 'I must' express Jesus' sense of relationship and responsibility to God, and His response to it."[89] The Boy Jesus experienced an urgency to be about His Father's mission for Him and seeks to express this divine relationship and unique call in His answer to Mary and Joseph. "At twelve years of age the eternal obligation to His mission came upon our Lord Jesus Christ."[90] Even at this early age,

---

[85] Luke 2:49b NASB.

[86] Anderson, *Gospel Firsts: Messages on the First Things in the Bible*, 47.

[87] Fitzmyer, "The Gospel According to Luke (I-IX)," 443.

[88] Hastings, *The Great Texts of the Bible: St. Luke*, 113.

[89] Anderson, *Gospel Firsts: Messages on the First Things in the Bible*, 43.

[90] Pentecost, *The Birth and Boyhood of Jesus*, 393.

Jesus understood His special relationship with God His Father and began to perceive His unique earthly task. "Jesus, then, would have his parents understand that he was in his Father's world among his Father's things, where was nothing to hurt him; he knew them all, was in the secret of them all, could use and order them as did his Father."[91]

The emerging consciousness of the Boy Jesus continued to grow and flourish. Jesus' twin questions to Mary and Joseph express three truths. First, Jesus understood His unique relationship with God the Father. "Here in Jerusalem, when only twelve years of age, the boy Jesus came to a personal realization of the character of God and of the claims which God had upon him."[92] Second, Jesus knew God intimately as His Father. For "there is in these words of Jesus, what was most characteristic in His consciousness, His conception of God as His Father."[93] Third, besides relating to God as a Son, Jesus understood His Father's particular call on His life and accepted his most holy mission. "Jesus felt Himself under an infinite compulsion to be about the things of His Father."[94] In these three ways, the Boy Jesus both expressed His relationship with God as Father and understood His unique divine mission.

Jesus' mission involved both total surrender and a passionate compulsion to fulfill the Father's will. Jesus first surrendered to this higher call. "Also in these words we find the boy-Jesus expressing a sweet 'must' of filial duty. He

---

[91] George MacDonald, *The Hope of the Gospel* (New York: Appleton, 1892), 58.

[92] Landrum, "Consecrated Childhood," 213.

[93] Garvie, *Studies in the Inner Life of Jesus*, 113.

[94] Baer, *The Old Gospel for the New Times*, 69.

was fully surrendered to His Father's will."[95] By seeking he friendly confines of the temple, the Boy Jesus expressed a desire to discern and execute God's will upon His young life. Second, within Jesus' heart, a sense of urgency propelled Him to humble obedience. "That little word, 'must,' reveals a passion and determination. There was an inner compulsion which was inextricable. It was the one paramount passion of His life, to fulfill the mission of the Father."[96] Even at the age of twelve, Jesus felt driven to answer His Father's call.

This sense of being driven began within the Boy Jesus' heart and did not spring from the outside. "In Jesus Christ the 'must' was not an external one, but He 'must be about His Father's business,' because His whole inclination and will was submitted to the Father's authority."[97] Although fluent in Sacred Scripture and articulate in answering the theological questions posed by the temple doctors, Jesus did not derive His mission apart from God the Father. This mission emerged in the deepest recesses of His heart where He intimately conversed with His heavenly Father.

The simple Greek word translated "must" or "had to be" offers valuable insight into Jesus' entire earthly ministry. At the most basic level, Jesus simply "had to be" in the temple during this Passover visit at the age of twelve. "By using the verb δει Luke makes Jesus' stay in the house of His Father a part of his ministry as a whole."[98] We cannot know with certainty whether Jesus visited the Jerusalem temple at an earlier age. Undoubtedly His inaugural Jerusalem journey

---

[95] Anderson, *Gospel Firsts: Messages on the First Things in the Bible*, 48.

[96] Colton, *Expository Studies in the Life of Christ*, 63.

[97] Maclaren, *After the Resurrection*, 199.

[98] Jonge, "Sonship, Wisdom, Infancy: Luke ii. 41-51a," 333.

would have been filled with joyful anticipation. Jesus would have heard about the temple from His parents and teachers and read about the temple in His study of Sacred Scripture. His young heart would beat with an inner urgency to be at the temple, within her walls, conversing with the learned doctors and asking them pertinent questions. This crucial first step in Jesus' public ministry foreshadows His full surrender to God's plan of salvation for humanity.

This memorable trip to the epicenter of Jewish worship begins a Scriptural journey of humble obedience to the will of His heavenly Father. Just as Jesus "had to be" in the temple, so too will He experience the "must" of innumerable events throughout the course of His earthly ministry. "But by using the verb δει Luke gives us to understand that Jesus' stay in the temple is to be understood as part of God's plan. This task will remain upon him until the ascension."[99] Jesus at the age of twelve makes His first recorded public appearance. "This is the first use of the impersonal δει, 'it is necessary,' in the Lucan Gospel."[100] Although all four gospel writers utilize this idea of necessity, Saint Luke in particular makes this a recurring theme throughout his Gospel account. "Δει referring to the necessity for Christ to fulfil God's plan is present in all four Gospels, but in the third it occurs so frequently that Hawkins characterized is as 'more or less characteristic of Luke.' "[101] A careful reading of Saint Luke's entire narrative leads to a most prevalent use of the word δει throughout various aspects of Jesus' public min-

....

[99] Ibid.

[100] Fitzmyer, "The Gospel According to Luke (I-IX)," 443.

[101] Jonge, "Sonship, Wisdom, Infancy: Luke ii. 41-51a," quoting John C. Hawkins, *Horae Synopticae: Contributions to the Study of the Synoptic Problem*, 2d ed. (Oxford: Clarendon, 1909), 24.

istry. This public ministry began in the temple at the age of twelve and incorporates God's entire plan of salvation. "It expresses not only a necessity in general, but the peculiar Lucan connotation of what had to be as part of the Father's salvific plan involving Jesus."[102]

Saint Luke's first use of δει introduces a major Lucan theme. "This great word 'must' is used about thirty times in the New Testament in relation to the mission of Christ, His work, His sufferings, His death, His resurrection, His ascension, His mediatorial sovereignty, and His final victory over sin and Satan, and the word proceeds mostly from the lips of Christ Himself."[103] The Boy Jesus at an early age expressed the inner compulsion of obedience to God. This urgent necessity permeated His entire time on earth:

Jesus' whole life was defined by this δει, from his first appearance as a twelve-year-old (ii. 49) to his death (xxii. 37), resurrection (Acts xvii. 3) and ascension (Acts iii. 21). This δει is based on God's decisions which are recorded in the Old Testament, cf. Luke xxiv. 44, "Everything written about me in the Law of Moses, the Prophets and Psalms, was bound to be fulfilled."[104]

Jesus felt compelled to be about the things and the places of His heavenly Father.

"This passage, with its humor and its humanness, carries us relentlessly toward the cross."[105] We only may speculate on Jesus' consciousness and comprehension of His inevitable walk to Calvary. Nearly two decades later, the Roman

---

[102] Fitzmyer, "The Gospel According to Luke (I-IX)," 443.

[103] Hastings, *The Great Texts of the Bible: St. Luke*, 132.

[104] Jonge, "Sonship, Wisdom, Infancy: Luke ii. 41-51a," 350-351.

[105] Chakoian, "Luke 2:41-52," 190.

procurator will condemn Jesus to death by cruel crucifixion. The Roman soldiers will nail His hands and His feet to the cross and pierce His side with a lance. One little Greek word first articulated by the Boy Jesus, δει, best expresses this lonely acceptance of a tortuous yet essential death.

> When He was hanging on the cross His enemies taunted Him with being an imposter and a false Christ, and challenged Him to prove His divine Sonship by coming down from the cross. What was it that held Him there? It was neither the nails that pierced His hands and feet, nor the thongs which bound Him to the cross. It was that eternal and blessed MUST. The Son of Man must suffer, or we must be lost.[106]

Jesus' perfect obedience to His heavenly Father ultimately sets us free.

With His first recorded words, the Boy Jesus both expresses His unique personal relationship with His heavenly Father and defines the underlying purpose of His life. "The passage cuts between our romantic expectations of what a perfect little boy might be, and the fanciful imagination of the apocryphal gospels, to this solid in-between: Jesus, coming of age, speaking with his own voice, in the Temple, about the claim God has on his life."[107] The Boy Jesus, united with His heavenly Father, begins His earthly mission with an inspired and obedient heart.

---

[106] Pentecost, *The Birth and Boyhood of Jesus*, 395.
[107] Chakoian, "Luke 2:41-52," 189.

CHAPTER SEVEN

FIVE GREEK WORDS

IT is a beauteous evening, calm and free,
The holy time is quiet as a Nun
Breathless with adoration; the broad sun
Is sinking down in its tranquility;
The gentleness of heaven broods o'er the Sea:
Listen! the mighty Being is awake,
And doth with his eternal motion make
A sound like thunder – everlastingly.
Dear Child! dear Girl! that walkest with me here,
If thou appear untouched by solemn thought,
Thy nature is not therefore less divine:
Thou liest in Abraham's bosom all the year;
And worship'st at the Temple's inner shrine,
God being with thee when we know it not.[108]

Translating the Greek of Jesus' first recorded words seems simple and straightforward but for five simple words. The precise interpretation of the short phrase εν τοις του πατρος μου continues to perplex Biblical scholars. Indeed, "the very climax of that story, i.e. the saying of Jesus in

---

[108] Wordsworth, " 'It is a Beauteous Evening, Calm and Free,'" 79.

2:49, seems ambiguous."[109] As a preview to determining the meaning and significance of these premier words of the Boy Jesus, this chapter will consider the five Greek words individually and as a phrase.

Biblical hermeneutics requires us to interpret these five Greek words within the context of the entire pericope. "Consider, for example, Luke's use of prepositional phrase introduced by *en* in 2:41-50. In five of the six instances other than 2:49 the sense is clearly spatial (2:43, 44, 44, 46, 46); but often it is much more."[110] These five passages will be considered in turn.

"As the story develops, Jesus is said to be 'in (*en*) Jerusalem' (2:43), while his parents are looking for him "in (*en*) the caravan ... among (*en*) their relatives and acquaintances' (2:44)."[111] These three references clearly demonstrate a spatial sense indicating place or location, yet a subtle distinction among the passages exists. Whereas the first phrase in 2:43 is primarily spatial, indicating the urban location of the Passover feast, the second and third passages in 2:44 add a personal element to the mix. "In this way Luke injects personal and dynamic quality to the sense of space in his narrative by describing a search among a group of fellow-pilgrims on their way home to Galilee from the Passover feast in Jerusalem (cf. 2:41-43)."[112] Although Saint Luke begins the pericope by expressing spatial location, the evangelist adds an interpersonal element to this by focusing the preposition εν upon people participating in the religious celebration.

---

[109] Francis D. Weinert, "The Multiple Meanings of Luke 2:49 and Their Significance," *Biblical Theology Bulletin* 13 (1983): 20.

[110] Ibid.

[111] Ibid.

[112] Ibid.

Saint Luke repeats the preposition εν twice in 2:46. As done earlier in this pericope, the evangelist aligns spatial preposition with an interpersonal one.

> In 2:46, Luke again uses two such prepositional phrases with much the same effect. There Jesus' parents, after returning to Jerusalem in search of their son, finally find him "sitting in (*en*) the Temple." Luke immediately amplifies the spatial sense of this phrase with greater dynamism and interpersonal import by adding "in (*en*) the midst of the teachers, listening to them and questioning them."[113]

Besides the clearly spatial and interpersonal uses of the preposition εν throughout this pericope, this last instance in the latter part of 2:46 adds a functional element as well. In this regard, Jesus not only visits the temple but also sits with the doctors in the temple; similarly, Jesus not only sits with the doctors, He also interacts with them by listening to their ideas and asking questions of them. "By the time Luke's readers reach the phrase *en tois tou patros mou* in 2:49, he already has conditioned them to think of Jesus' location, particularly when he is in the Temple, in personal and functional terms as well."[114]

The first word in εν τοις του πατρος μου, though primarily spatial in orientation, expresses interpersonal and functional elements as well. An interpretation of this preposition meaning "in" seems relatively simple. Similarly, analyzing the final three Greek words in the phrase – του πατρος μου – leads to

---

[113] Ibid.

[114] Ibid., 21.

several similar translations, from "my Father's"[115] to "of my Father."[116] Thus the interpretation of four of the five Greek words in the phrase εν τοις του πατρος μου appears quite straightforward. The Greek word τοις, however, proves to be very problematic.

This problem arises while attempting to translate τοις, the second Greek word in the five-word phrase. "The ambiguity results from Luke's use of the plural article *tois* without an immediately corresponding noun, something which he evidently expects his reader to supply."[117] The Greek τοις, a dative plural article, does not directly represent a specific noun. In other words, "the Greek, taken literally, says, 'Wist ye not that I must be in the – of my Father?' The authorized version supplies *business*; the revised, *house*. There is no noun in the Greek, and the article 'the' is in the plural."[118] Biblical scholars continue to disagree as to what noun is to follow the Greek definite article τοις in Luke 2:49.

Τοις may be either neuter or masculine.

> The dative plural article *tois* in the phrase *en tois tou patros mou*, if read as neuter, could designate either the temple precincts or *ta erga tou theou*, i.e. "God's great and marvelous deeds;" and if it read as masculine, it may

---

[115] Kendrick, *The Moral Conflict of Humanity and Other Papers*, 136; Spurgeon, *C.H. Spurgeon's Sermons on Crises in the Life of* Jesus, 13.

[116] Hastings, *The Great Texts of the Bible: St. Luke*, 107.

[117] Weinert, "The Multiple Meanings of Luke 2:49 and Their Significance," 19.

[118] MacDonald, *The Hope of the Gospel*, 46.

> even refer to the teachers among whom Jesus has just been found sitting in dialogue.[119]

Depending upon whether τοις is masculine or neuter, this definite article may represent one of all three types of noun forms: person, place, or thing.

Simply stated, the Greek phrase εν τοις του πατρος μου offers a myriad of meanings. "The Greek is not absolutely clear."[120] Most scholars have taken an "either-or" rather than a "both-and" approach to this dilemma, firmly expressing one interpretation to the exclusion of all others. "It is remarkable to note how many participants in the debate have opted very decisively for one or other extreme viewpoint."[121] Rather than seeking consensus with the hope of discovering an acceptable middle ground, many Biblical scholars find themselves either at one extreme or the other.

> We may confine ourselves to mentioning two views which are difficult to reconcile. B. S. Easton wrote that έν τοις τλκ "can mean only 'in my Father's house.'" J. A. Scott on the other hand wrote that the same words "can mean only 'in the affairs of my Father' or 'things of my Father.'"[122]

Rather than offer a variety of possible meanings, these two scholars promote only one interpretation in exclusive terms, hence prohibiting a combination of possibilities.

---

[119] Weinert, "The Multiple Meanings of Luke 2:49 and Their Significance," 21.

[120] MacDonald, *The Hope of the Gospel*, 41.

[121] Jonge, "Sonship, Wisdom, Infancy: Luke ii. 41-51a," 331.

[122] Ibid.

While some scholars offer divergent interpretations, others express why a particular meaning must by necessity be erroneous. For example, "Laurentin too allowed himself to be tempted to write 'the expression ειναι ἐν τοίς τού (followed by a personal name) never meant 'to be occupied in the affairs of and could not be understood in that sense.'"[123] While one Biblical scholar postulates a precise meaning for the Greek phrase in question, another indicates this could not possibly be the case.

The Greek phrase in question refutes an easy explanation. In the following example, another Biblical scholar offers several possible interpretations:

> To translate it as literally as it can be translated, making of it an English sentence, the saying stands, "Wist ye not that I must be in the things of my Father?" The plural article implies the English "things"; and the question is then, What things does He mean? The word might mean affairs or business. On the other hand we might translate, "Wist ye not that I must be in my Father's?" Then, in almost all languages "house" would be understood. We commonly say to one another, "I am going down to my father's," or "I shall spend the evening at my brother's." Everybody knows that we mean "house," and that is just how the Greek here runs.[124]

This succinct summary shows the depth and breadth of possible scenarios.

....

[123] Ibid.
[124] Hastings, *The Great Texts of the Bible: St. Luke*, 107.

Rather than focusing on divergent views, some Biblical scholars try to reconcile competing interpretations.

> Now, the last words of this question are in the Greek literally, as the margin of the Revised Version tells us, "in the things of My Father"; and that idiomatic form of speech may either be taken to mean, as the Authorized Version does, "about My Father's business," or, with the Revised Version, "in My Father's house".[125]

In this analysis, both "business" and "house" fall within the idiomatic expression "in the things of My Father." Faced with these two distinct words, neither of which appears in the text, a Biblical scholar may compare and contrast the distinct possibilities before seeking a "both-and" solution.

> The latter seems the rendering most relevant in this connection, where the folly of seeking is emphasized — the certainty of His place is more to the point than that of His occupation. But the locality carried the occupation with it, for why must He be in the Father's house but to be about the Father's business, "to behold the beauty of the Lord and to inquire in His temple"?[126]

According to this scholar, Saint Luke expresses both "house" and "business" despite the absence of both words within this most pertinent Greek phrase.

Given the centuries-old confusion as to the meaning of Jesus' first recorded words, one may question why scholars

....

[125] Maclaren, *After the Resurrection*, 198.
[126] Ibid.

even bother to pinpoint a precise interpretation. In this regard, these first words express a deep and abiding relevancy regardless of their exact meaning. "The discovery that Jesus is now old enough to call God his Father and the temple his Father's house and God's worship his own business has all the force of shock. "Wist ye not that I must be in my Father's house and about my Father's business?' It was a stunning question."[127]

Saint Luke could have recorded a variety of experiences and words from Jesus' first three decades on earth. That the evangelist chose this particular setting, Jesus' visit to the Jerusalem temple at the age of twelve, and recorded two specific questions conversing with His Mother Mary, leads most scholars to acknowledge the significant relevance of this most precious pericope.

The task facing the Biblical scholar seeking to interpret εν τοις του πατρος μου accurately seems especially insurmountable. Saint Luke clearly states Mary and Joseph failed to comprehend Jesus' first recorded words. "But they did not understand the statement which He spoke to them."[128] Standing right before their Son in the temple precincts, Jesus asked two questions, and Mary and Joseph did not understand what He meant. "His parents had his exact words, yet did not understand. We have not his exact words, and are in doubt as to what the Greek translation of them means."[129]

Despite this uncertainty and confusion, Jesus' meaning expressed in Luke 2:49 may still be understood. Although Mary and Joseph "did not understand the statement which

---

[127] Landrum, "Consecrated Childhood," 218.

[128] Luke 2:50 NKJV.

[129] MacDonald, *The Hope of the Gospel*, 42.

He had made to them,"[130] this same lack of comprehension does not automatically transfer to Saint Luke's readers past and present. If we can discern the precise meaning of εν τοις του πατρος μου, we successfully escape and even transcend the Holy Family's pronounced perplexity.

The proper interpretation of Luke 2:49 depends upon how one translates εν τοις του πατρος μου. In this regard, "the interpretation of Luke 2:49 is tied quite closely to one's translation of that text, and especially of the prepositional phrase en tois tou patros mou, i.e. '(in/about) the (things/people/precincts) of my Father.'"[131] The prepositional phrase begins with εν, variously translated as either "in" or "about." The plural article τοις stands by itself, with no explicit noun following, leading different Biblical scholars to substitute "things," "people," or "precincts" for the missing word. Regardless of how we translate this prepositional phrase, the eternal interconnectedness with God as Jesus' heavenly Father remains certain.

These three possibilities – things, people, and precincts – correspond well to the classic definition of a noun as being a person ("people"), a place ("precincts"), or a thing ("things"). Although Mary and Joseph failed to understand the Boy Jesus' two questions, the missing noun following εν τοις automatically does not engender confusion to the reader of Saint Luke's succinct account. Clarity replaces confusion to the extent Biblical scholars solve the dilemma of the missing noun and present an intelligent interpretation of εν τοις του πατρος μου.

---

[130] Luke 2:50 NASB.

[131] Weinert, "The Multiple Meanings of Luke 2:49 and Their Significance," 19.

One Biblical scholar from France compiled all the various interpretations in one book. "A survey of the solutions given by old and new translations, the fathers and the commentaries, can be found in Laurentin."[132] René Laurentin authored the seminal work on this dilemma.[133] Specifically, this French scholar describes five possible interpretations of the missing noun following εν τοις. First, "*Choses*"[134] as things; second, "*Personnes*"[135] as people; third, "*Domaine*"[136] as field or sphere; fourth, "*Affaires*"[137] as businesses or concerns; and fifth, "*Maison ou demeure*" as house.[138]

With an eye to Laurentin yet also considering theories advanced since completion of his seminal work, we see six distinct yet interrelated interpretations of εν τοις του πατρος μου: the three parts of a noun (person, place, thing) and three other unique exegetical interpretations (ambivalence, integration, pilgrimage). These six theories will be considered in-depth and in turn.

---

[132] Jonge, "Sonship, Wisdom, Infancy: Luke ii. 41-51a," 331.
[133] Laurentin, *Jésus au Temple* (Paris: Gabalda, 1966).
[134] Ibid., 39.
[135] Ibid., 42.
[136] Ibid., 46.
[137] Ibid., 47.
[138] Ibid., 56.

CHAPTER EIGHT

THEORY ONE: PERSON

Most High, all-powerful, good Lord,
Yours are the praises, the glory, the honor, and all blessing.
To You alone, Most High, do they belong,
and no man is worthy to mention Your name.
Praised be You, my Lord, with all your creatures,
especially Sir Brother Sun,
Who is the day and through whom You give us light.
And he is beautiful and radiant with great splendor;
and bears a likeness of You, Most High One.
Praised be You, my Lord, through Sister Moon and the stars,
in heaven You formed them clear and precious and beautiful.
Praised be You, my Lord, through Brother Wind,
and through the air, cloudy and serene, and every kind of weather
through which You give sustenance to Your creatures.
Praised be You, my Lord, through Sister Water,
which is very useful and humble and precious and chaste.
Praised be You, my Lord, through Brother Fire,
through whom You light the night
and he is beautiful and playful and robust and strong.
Praised be You, my Lord, through our Sister Mother Earth,
who sustains and governs us,
and who produces varied fruits with colored flowers and herbs.

> Praised be You, my Lord, through those who give pardon for
>   Your love
> and bear infirmity and tribulation.
> Blessed are those who endure in peace
> for by You, Most High, they shall be crowned.
> Praised be You, my Lord, through our Sister Bodily Death,
> from whom no living man can escape.
> Woe to those who die in mortal sin.
> Blessed are those whom death will find in Your most holy will,
> for the second death shall do them no harm.
> Praise and bless my Lord and give Him thanks
> and serve Him with great humility.[139]

The preposition εν and definite article τοις may refer to one or more persons. Laurentin asserts the phrase εν τοις του πατρος μου "can mean only 'with my Father' and nothing else."[140] In adhering to this view, Laurentin relies upon the verb δει, meaning "must," to portend Christ's future glorification. As one Biblical scholar quotes Laurentin:

> Jesus would have said, "I must be with my Father", meaning by this, "I must come by suffering and resurrection to share the glory of my Father in heaven". Jesus' words in ii. 49 would thus have been a mysterious prediction of his resurrection and exaltation. Laurentin draws this conclusion from the fact that the verb δει is used, which in his opinion is "l'expression-cle pour signifier le mystere pascal."[141]

---

[139] Saint Francis of Assisi, "The Canticle of Brother Sun," 38-39.
[140] Jonge, "Sonship, Wisdom, Infancy: Luke ii. 41-51a," 336.
[141] Ibid.

Contrary to this view, the verb δει is used many other times in Saint Luke's Gospel, and sometimes such use does not coincide with Jesus' death and resurrection. "Luke thus did not use the verb exclusively to indicate that it was God's will that Jesus should suffer, die and be resurrected."[142] One wonders whether the Boy Jesus would have made such a bold and prophetic proclamation absent more textual evidence of such a mysterious intent.

God the Father may not be the only person intended to be reflected by the clause εν τοις. One translation focuses upon the household or relatives of Jesus' heavenly Father. This interpretation cites contextual evidence within the larger pericope to Mary and Joseph's search among their relatives and acquaintances. After a day's journey, "they began looking for Him among their relatives and acquaintances."[143] This connection between earthly and heavenly acquaintances involves a slight contextual shift:

> "In or among the household (relatives) of my (heavenly) Father." The Lucan context where the parents had searched for Jesus among their relatives and acquaintances (*en tois syngeneusin*), and therefore among the household of Jesus' earthly father, makes appropriate supplying *a noun naming persons*. In reply to his parents' search Jesus could be conceived as telling them that they should have searched among the relatives or household of his heavenly Father (*en tois tou patros mou*).[144]

---

[142] Ibid.

[143] Luke 2:44b NASB.

[144] Brown, *The Birth of the Messiah*, 476 (emphasis in original).

The temple doctors similarly would be associated with God the Father. In this regard, εν τοις του πατρος μου might mean " 'among those people belonging to my Father,' if *tois* were understood as masc. pl., i.e. among the teachers of the Torah."[145]

Critics assail this connection between the temple doctors and God the Father. "The insurmountable obstacle to this interpretation is the impossibility that Jesus would have spoken of the teachers of the Law in the Temple as 'the household (family) of my Father.'"[146] Jesus' intimate and personal relationship with His Father, not the lively interplay of ideas with the teachers, makes this pericope special.

An unnamed noun follows the preposition εν and the plural article τοις. The presence of του πατρος μου brings the Father into the picture but does not resolve the dilemma of the missing noun following εν τοις.

---

[145] Fitzmyer, "The Gospel According to Luke (I-IX)," 443.
[146] Brown, *The Birth of the Messiah*, 477.

CHAPTER NINE

THEORY TWO: PLACE

PURE fasted faces draw unto this feast:
God comes all sweetness to your Lenten lips.
You striped in secret with breath-taking whips,
Those crooked rough-scored chequers may be pieced
To crosses meant for Jesus; you whom the East
With draught of thin and pursuant cold so nips
Breathe Easter now; you serged fellowships,
You vigil-keepers with low flames decreased,

God shall o'er-brim the measures you have spent
With oil of gladness; for sackcloth and frieze
And the ever-fretting shirt of punishment
Give myrrhy-threaded golden folds of ease.
Your scarce-sheathed bones are weary of being bent:
Lo, God shall strengthen all the feeble knees.[147]

Besides denoting a person, the noun associated with εν τοις may designate a particular place. "The phrase 'in my Father's house' is the most acceptable translation for the words en tois tou patros mou."[148] A variety of sources sup-

---

[147] Hopkins, "Easter Communion," *Poems of Gerard Manley Hopkins*, 35.

[148] Kilgallen, "Luke 2, 41-50: Foreshadowing of Jesus, Teacher,"

port this interpretation. "This translation is supported by the Syriac, Armenian, and Persian versions, by the Greek Church fathers, and by many of the Latin fathers, following Augustine."[149] As noted by one Biblical scholar, "In support of the version that I have preferred, 'in my Father's house' (= chez mon Père), a number of instances have been found in biblical and extrabiblical Greek texts of the neut. pl. of the def. art. followed by a gen. (sg. or pl.) in the sense of the 'house/household of X.'"[150] The translation "in my Father's house" seems well-established in both Biblical and non-Biblical sources.

"The Greek *en tois tou patros mou* is literally 'in the ... of my father,' with the plural of the definite article used instead of a specific substantive."[151] Another reason for designating "house" as the unnamed noun arises from contextual considerations. "La plupart des exègétes se rallient aujourd'hui à la seconde parce qu'elle cadre mieux avec le contexte de l'épisode."[152] In other words, "(t)he majority of the exegetes adopt ('in my Father's house') today because it rallies better with the context of the episode."

Studying the pericope as a whole, one sees Mary and Joseph journeying place to place in the hope of finding Jesus. "What seems to favor most the translation 'in my Father's house' from an internal point of view is that Jesus's parents are consistently pictured as looking *where* to find him."[153]

....
556.

[149] Brown, *The Birth of the Messiah*, 476.

[150] Fitzmyer, "The Gospel According to Luke (I-IX)," 443.

[151] Brown, *The Birth of the Messiah*, 475.

[152] Laurentin, *Structure et Théologie de Luc I – II* (Paris: Gabalda, 1957), 143.

[153] Kilgallen, "Luke 2, 41-50: Foreshadowing of Jesus, Teacher," 556

The pericope's central problem involves the lost Boy Jesus. Similarly, the resolution of this problem involves the parents finding Jesus somewhere. "Thus, the manner of addressing the problem and the description of its resolution suggest that 'place', and the search for it, is a main concern and that this central concern is relieved in the finding of Jesus 'in my Father's house.'"[154]

Contextual considerations support "place" as the essential ingredient following the preposition εν and the plural definite article τοις. " 'In the dwelling-place (house) of my (heavenly) Father.' The Lucan context where the parents are searching for Jesus makes appropriate supplying *a noun of locale*. The neuter plural of the definite article with the preposition *en* is well attested in the meaning 'in the dwelling-place of,'"[155] with such an emphasis found in Biblical and non-Biblical sources. As one scholar notes, "Luke's Greek phrase would then have the sense of the French *chez*. The more specific identification of 'place' as 'house' is encouraged by the fact that Jesus is in the Temple, which on several occasions is referred to as God's house (*oikos*); see Luke 19:46; John 2:16 ('my Father's house').[156] In addition, " 'My Father's house' seems also most relevant in this connexion, where the folly of seeking is emphasized – the certainty of His place is more to the point than that of His occupation."[157] Within the context of the Holy Family's search for the Boy Jesus, "in

---

(emphasis in original).

[154] Ibid., 557.

[155] Brown, *The Birth of the Messiah*, 475 (emphasis in original).

[156] Ibid., 476.

[157] Hastings, *The Great Texts of the Bible: St. Luke*, 107-108.

my Father's house" seems like an appropriate interpretation of εν τοις του πατρος μου.

As indicated earlier, "Christ's name for the Temple was 'my Father's house.' This makes the translation 'in my Father's house' the more natural thing for Him to say."[158] Rejecting the other widespread interpretation involving "my Father's business," the translation "my Father's house" appears simpler, a phrase more likely to be uttered by a child of twelve. "But, further, we feel that the words are more natural, because they are more child-like. It is hardly the saying of a child that He must be about the concerns or affairs or businesses of His father."[159] Whereas "business" denotes an adult level of sophistication, "house" seems to be a simple yet concise word both describing place and respecting the speaker's young age.

Although the temple as God's house suggests something sublime, this reference also may be the most basic destination of a devoted twelve-year-old boy's Passover visit to the Jerusalem center of worship. "From the moment of his unannounced departure from them, the only place he could have been was the Temple, the house of his Father. They could have found him there without the trouble of looking elsewhere."[160] Had they paused to consider, Mary and Joseph's return journey to Jerusalem would have progressed in the calm assurance of success, as the Boy Jesus, devoted to His heavenly Father, could be found nowhere else. "So understood, his answer is, at first glance, less sublime; but

---

[158] Ibid., 116.

[159] Ibid.

[160] Prat, *Jesus Christ: His Life, His Teaching, and His Work*, 123.

how much more natural on the lips of a child, who utters it with a caress and a smile."[161]

The concept of place, specifically delineated in the phrase, "in my Father's house," seems to be the leading interpretation advanced by most Biblical scholars and translations. Many critics, however, disagree with this assessment.

"Yet it must be stressed that if Luke had only wanted to say, 'I must be in my Father's house', he expressed himself in an unnatural and even extraordinary manner."[162] Later in his Gospel account, the evangelist writes, "And he went into the temple, and began to cast out them that sold therein, and them that bought; Saying unto them, It is written, My house is the house of prayer: but ye have made it a den of thieves."[163] In the original Greek of this text, Saint Luke wrote the word οικος when referring to God's house. "But the problem is this: if Luke does not hesitate to call the Temple God's 'house' (*oikos*) in 19:46, why does he omit this word in favor of the more indirect expression in 2:49?"[164]

Jesus uses the word οικος to describe "my Father's house" in Luke 19:46. Yet this same Greek word decidedly is absent in Luke 2:49. "When, according to the Greek, the Lord, on the occasion already alluded to, says 'my Father's house,' he says it plainly; he uses the word *house*: here he does not."[165] The absence of οικος in Luke 2:49 leads scholars to question whether the concept of "house" is the missing noun intended to follow the preposition and definite article εν τοις.

---

[161] Ibid.

[162] Jonge, "Sonship, Wisdom, Infancy: Luke ii. 41-51a," 332.

[163] Luke 19:45-46 KJV.

[164] Weinert, "The Multiple Meanings of Luke 2:49 and Their Significance," 19.

[165] MacDonald, *The Hope of the Gospel*, 46 (emphasis in original).

Luke 19:46 is not the only example in Saint Luke's Gospel of Jesus' use of οικος to describe His Father's house. In the parable of the rich man and Lazarus, Jesus speaks for the rich man: "Then he said, I pray thee therefore, father, that thou wouldest send him to my father's house: For I have five brethren; that he may testify unto them, lest they also come into this place of torment."[166] For the prepositional phrase "to my father's house," Jesus again uses the Greek οικος.

As one scholar asserts, Saint Luke often uses οικος to describe a house. A form of οικος is used in Luke 19:5 to refer to Zaccheus' house. All the Gospel writers use οικος to refer to God's house or the temple (Matthew 23:35, Mark 2:26, Mark 11:17, Luke 6:4, Luke 11:51, John 2:16).[167]

Why would Jesus refer to "my Father's house" in Luke 2:49 without adding οικος? This perplexing question arises because to do so would have been quite simple. "Luke's choice of words is *unnatural*, because for 'my Father's house' he could simply have written ο οικος του πατρος μου, just as in xvi. 27."[168] Biblical scholars must acknowledge the translation "in my Father's house," absent the Greek οικος, is at best indirect.

> The climax of the story and the core of this biographical apothegm comes at the end of Jesus' second question: "Did you not know that *I must be in my Father's house?*" In the NOTE I have defended this translation of an ambiguous Greek expression; here I would stress only that

....

[166] Luke 16:27-28 KJV.

[167] Jonge, "Sonship, Wisdom, Infancy: Luke ii. 41-51a," 332.

[168] Ibid., (emphasis in original).

the word "house" does not occur in the Greek so that the reference to the Temple is at most indirect.[169]

Critics question how scholars can compare Luke 2:49 with other Gospel verses where οικος is present. Consider, for example, John 2:16: "And said unto them that sold doves, Take these things hence; make not my Father's house an house of merchandise."[170]

> This means that Laurentin and others are wrong when they draw a close parallel between this saying and that of John 2:16: "You shall not make my Father's house a house of business." There precisely Jesus does use the word "house" to stress the nature of the Temple, and the statement is part of the prophetic stance of Jesus in the ministry reinterpreting the cult.[171]

Contrast this to Luke 2:49, with its emphasis upon God as Jesus' heavenly Father, not the temple as God's house. "Here he is not reinterpreting the Temple as his Father's house. He is merely saying that his presence in the Temple and his listening to the teachers is indicative of where his vocation lies, namely, in the service of God who is his Father, not at the beck and call of his natural family."[172]

Despite these legitimate criticisms of the translation "in my Father's house," some scholars explain the absence of οικος as in no way prohibiting an understanding of "house."

---

[169] Brown, *The Birth of the Messiah*, 490 (emphasis in original).
[170] John 2:16 KJV.
[171] Brown, *The Birth of the Messiah*, 490.
[172] Ibid.

In these instances, the word "house" is not included in the precise translation but implied. " 'Knew ye not that I must be at my Father's?' So I translate, in accordance with a majority of the best ancient and modern interpretations."[173] These precious words Mary and Joseph would not yet understand; the Boy Jesus, intimately associated with His heavenly Father, would so comprehend.

---

[173] Kendrick, *The Moral Conflict of Humanity and Other Papers*, 136.

CHAPTER TEN

THEORY THREE: THING

As kingfishers catch fire, dragonflies dráw flame;
As tumbled over rim in roundy wells
Stones ring; like each tucked string tells, each hung bell's
Bow swung finds tongue to fling out broad its name;
Each mortal thing does one thing and the same:
Deals out that being indoors each one dwells;
Selves—goes itself; *myself* it speaks and spells;
Crying *Whát I dó is me: for that I came.*

Í say more: the just man justices;
Kéeps gráce: thát keeps all his goings graces;
Acts in God's eye what in God's eye he is—
Christ—for Christ plays in ten thousand places,
Lovely in limbs, and lovely in eyes not his
To the Father through the features of men's faces.[174]

Were the Boy Jesus merely describing His location in the temple to His parents, He could have communicated this point clearly. In this regard, the mysterious absence of a noun after εν τοις continues to baffle.

---

[174] Hopkins, *Poems of Gerard Manley Hopkins*, 95 (emphasis in original).

Indeed, there is the oddity of the phrase *en tois tou patrou*; though parallels are to be found in literature which justify the translation, "in the house of ... ", such a parallel is not found in the rest of the Lucan work, whereas in the very same Finding in the Temple story there is the clear and simple usage *en toi hieroi* (v. 46).[175]

Had Jesus wanted to indicate location, He could have accomplished this with both simplicity and clarity.

"Yet, for all the internal indication about the importance of 'place', one wonders whether or not there is something more than just 'place' to consider here. First, Mary's opening question to her child is expressed with emphasis on cause: 'Why did you treat us in this way?' "[176] The Virgin Mary found the Boy Jesus in the temple; she seeks an explanation as to the rationale for His separation and His parent's subsequent search. "What is on her mind then is not only where the lost Jesus is, but what could have led him to separate himself from his parents."[177] The place or location of Jesus in the temple, though contextually adequate, raises more questions than it answers. In this regard, "though the translation 'in my Father's house' does justice to the primary concern about the 'lostness' of Jesus and 'where' he is to be found, it is not adequate to answer the question, why is Jesus willing to disrupt things so as to spend time in his true Father's house?"[178]

....

[175] Kilgallen, "Luke 2, 41-50: Foreshadowing of Jesus, Teacher," 557.

[176] Ibid.

[177] Ibid.

[178] Ibid.

This question leads to a shift in consideration from place to thing. " 'In or about the things (business, affairs) of my (heavenly) Father.' The Lucan context where Jesus is found in the Temple precincts 'seated in the midst of the teachers, both listening to them and asking them questions,' makes appropriate supplying *a noun of activity*."[179] Whereas "house" indicates location, "things, business, affairs" denotes activity.

> There is nothing in Jesus' divine sonship that should have led his parents to know where he would be (i.e., in the Temple precincts). But conceivably, knowing that he was God's Son, the parents could have known that he would be involved in God's affairs, e.g., by discussing the Law and asking religious questions; and so they should not have worried. This logic is a bit forced, and the grammatical basis is weaker than for the previous explanation.[180]

Although admittedly weak, the translation for supplying "business" as the missing noun after εν τοις has advocates. "Though the translation which mentions business may be a questionable one, yet it is abundantly lawful to say that this holy child's occupation was to be about his Father's matters."[181] The original Greek doesn't seem to capture the depth of heart actively exerted by the Boy Jesus in the temple:

> This holy child is about his Father's business, for *he is engrossed in it*. His whole heart is in the hearing and

---

[179] Brown, *The Birth of the Messiah*, 476 (emphasis in original).

[180] Ibid.

[181] Spurgeon, *C.H. Spurgeon's Sermons on Crises in the Life of Jesus*, 16.

> asking questions. There is a force, to my mind, in the Greek, which is lost in the translation, which drags in the word "*about*". There is nothing parallel to it in the Greek, which is, "Wist ye not know that I must be in my Father's?" The way to worship God is to get heartily into it."[182]

The translation "about my Father's business" also faces strong criticism. In this regard, a twelve-year-old boy would not be likely to explain His disappearance in this way.

> The rendering of the common version, "about my Father's business," is indeed, grammatically, equally defensible, but much less intrinsically probable. That the child of twelve years should chide his parents for seeking him, on the ground that he ought to be engaged in the business of his Father, is scarcely natural, especially when we remember that he immediately returned home with them, and remained in retirement and subjection until his thirtieth year.[183]

If the Boy Jesus truly felt compelled to be "about my Father's business" in the temple, why would He so readily abandon this mission in return home to Nazareth in obedience?

The critique of "business" as the appropriate interpretation does not necessarily extend to "things." To insert the general concept of "things" after εν τοις εν τοις seems to make more sense. "To translate it as literally as it can be translated, making of it an English sentence, the saying

---

[182] Ibid., 17-18 (emphasis in original).

[183] Kendrick, *The Moral Conflict of Humanity and Other Papers*, 136.

stands, 'Wist ye not that I must be in the things of my Father?' "[184] The conclusion may be preferable to translations advocating that Jesus be about the business or affairs of His Father.

Although these traditional translations may be defended, they appear limited when contrasted with the word "things."

> The translation given in the authorized version is, I think, as to the words themselves, a thoroughly justifiable one: "I must be about my Father's business," or "my Father's affairs."; I refuse it for no other reason than that it does not fit the logic of the narrative, as does the word *things*, which besides opens to us a door of large and joyous prospect."[185]

The concept of "things" implies no limitation. Whereas "business" and "affairs" are specific, the plural "things" remains general, therefore offering the reader a wider variety of possibilities.

"The words 'I must' expresses His sense of relationship and responsibility to God, and His response to it."[186] Literally translated, εν τοις του πατρος μου may be best understood if "things" follows εν τοις: "In the Greek the form is, 'I must be in the things of the Father of me.' "[187] In other words, after "person" and "place," the third general category of a noun, "thing," best incorporates the myriad of meaning the Boy Jesus sought to express.

....

[184] MacDonald, *The Hope of the Gospel*, 46.

[185] Ibid., 47-48 (emphasis in original).

[186] Anderson, *Gospel Firsts: Messages on the First Things in the Bible*, 43.

[187] Ibid.

Besides "business" or "things," "affairs" may fit better within the context of Luke 2:49. According to one Biblical scholar, "it is most likely that the Boy of twelve spoke the language of His own home."[188] If this is the case, the Boy Jesus would have addressed the Blessed Virgin Mary and Joseph in either Aramaic or Hebrew. This possibility argues against the use of the word "house" within the pericope. "If Luke is giving us a literal translation of Jesus' words, then the odds are against 'house,' for in Hebrew or Aramaic the word 'house' is not eclipsed."[189]

> Luke preserves Hebrew or Aramaic style in this whole section (indeed it is fairly well proven that here he faithfully followed a Hebrew or less likely an Aramaic original), and if his indefinite expression is for the purpose of preserving an original indefinite expression, this indefiniteness suggest "affairs."[190]

Given that most scholars debate whether the proper missing noun after εν τοις is either "house" or "business," this scholar concludes "the view of 'business' is to be preferred: 'I must be in the affairs of My Father,' or as the ordinary reading runs: 'I must be about My Father's business.' "[191]

Regardless of the precise interpretation of the noun form of "things," the depth of meaning behind Jesus' first recorded words reaches as far as the universe expands and beyond. "All His life He was among His Father's things, either in

---

[188] Temple, "What is to be understood by *En Tois* Luke 2, 49?", 259.
[189] Ibid.
[190] Ibid., 259-260.
[191] Ibid., 260.

heaven or in the world – not only then when they found Him in the Temple at Jerusalem. He is still among His Father's things, everywhere about in the world, everywhere throughout the wide universe."[192] Such an interpretation, though exciting in its scope, seems unduly restricted to the context of the pericope: Mary and Joseph found Jesus in the temple. His reality leads some Biblical scholars to define εν τοις του πατρος μου beyond person, place, or thing, suggesting a combination of two or more of these concepts.

To introduce this possibility and perhaps better explain Jesus' absence and separation, Biblical scholars point to a higher purpose beyond the Boy's mere presence in the temple. In doing so, they combine the concepts of person, place and thing into various combinations. This next three chapters will consider these combinations and three additional interpretive theories under the headings of ambivalence, integration, and pilgrimage, respectively.

---

[192] Hastings, *The Great Texts of the Bible: St. Luke*, 121.

CHAPTER ELEVEN

THEORY FOUR: AMBIVALENCE

"Man of Song and Man of Science,
Truly you are as people on the outside of a house,
And one of you sees only that it is made of stone, and its windows of glass, and that fire burns in the hearth,
And the other of you sees that the house is beautiful and very human,
But I have gone inside the house,
And I live with the host in that house
And I have broken bread with him, and drunk his wine,
And seen the transfiguration that love and awe make in the brain . . .
For that house is the world, and the Lord is my host and my Father:
It is my Father's house. . . .
Enough? I see what is enough!
Machinery is enough for a Scientist,
And Beauty is enough for a Poet;
But in the hearts of men and women, and in the thirsty hearts of little children
There is a hunger, and there is an unappeasable longing,
For a Father and for the love of a Father . . .
For the root of a soul is mystery,
And the Night is mystery,

And in that mystery men and women open inward into Eternity,
And know love, the Lord.
Blessed be his works, and his angels, and his sons crowned with his glory!"[193]

A theory of deliberate ambivalence seeks to merge more than one element of person, place, or thing in the Boy Jesus' first recorded words. According to this theory, Saint Luke the evangelist purposely left the phrase εν τοις του πατρος μου ambiguous in order to allow for a variety of expressions.

> The words εν τοις του πατρος μου in Luke ii. 49 can therefore mean "in my Father's house" and as appears from the way in which the fathers understood this passage, they naturally have this meaning in the context in which they occur. As appears from analogous expressions in early Christian literature, however, Luke's phrase can also be given another and more general meaning. The question is therefore justified whether in Luke ii. 49 the interpretation "the things of" does not make enough sense for it to be concluded that Luke deliberately chose an enigmatic expression in order to profit from its ambivalence. This is indeed the case, for several reasons.[194]

---

[193] James Oppenheim, "My Father's House," quoted in *The Questing Spirit: Religion in the Literature of Our Time*, edited by Halford E. Luccock and Frances Brentano (New York: Coward-McCann, 1947), 313-314.

[194] Jonge, "Sonship, Wisdom, Infancy: Luke ii. 41-51a," 333.

These reasons will be considered in turn.

The ambivalent theory developed because no single translation of εν τοις του πατρος μου proves to be adequate. "The ambivalence of the sentence εν τοις του πατρος μου δει με ειναι is probably not susceptible of a satisfactory rendering in any language."[195] Faced with this language inadequacy, a translator often chooses an "either-or" rather than a "both-and" solution. "The translator is therefore faced with the problem of which of the two meanings he is to choose."[196] Many translators, unable to fully embrace one possible rendering, propose one interpretation in the text and another in a footnote. "The least inadequate solution is to give one version in the text, and refer in a note to the deliberate ambivalence and the alternative meaning. Several translations give a footnote at ii. 49, to indicate another translation is possible. This, however, is not enough."[197] This duality fails to adequately weigh several distinct possibilities naturally arising from Luke's deliberate use of an ambiguous phrase.

Rather than accept one possible translation while rejecting another, Biblical scholars may choose to incorporate a more general term capable of a wider breadth of meaning.

> Attention has to be drawn to the fact that both translations correspond to Luke's intention. If no note can be given, "I must concern myself with the things of my Father" should be preferred, as the intention which it

---

[195] Ibid., 335.

[196] Ibid.

[197] Ibid.

expresses could not adequately be grasped by a reader who saw only "I must be in my Father's house".[198]

Such a translation avoids the limitations imposed by utilizing specific terms like "house" or "business."

Instead of just settling for a more all-encompassing word, Biblical scholars go a step further in describing the ambivalence in the Boy Jesus' first recorded words as intentional. "The expression εν τοις του πατρος μου is deliberately ambivalent."[199] These scholars combine two possible scenarios into one cohesive whole. "Within the context of the episode ii. 41-51, it means 'in the house of my Father', yet *at the same time* it has a meaning which goes beyond the episode: Jesus is depicted as being involved in his Father's plans and their realization."[200] To limit the ambiguous phrase narrowly ignores the possibility of a predetermined ambivalence. "Clearly, εν τοις του πατρος μου means not only 'in the house of my Father', but also εν οις ο πατηρ μου διεθετο, that is, in the work that my Father's plan and decision imply."[201]

This solution allows the Boy Jesus to return to Nazareth in obedience rather than remain at the Jerusalem temple as the only place He must (δει) be. "There is yet another reason why it is necessary to interpret the words εν τοις του πατρος μου as ambivalent. Ancient readers immediately understood the text in the sense, 'I must be in the temple', but in 51 Luke

---

[198] Ibid., 335-336.

[199] Ibid., 353.

[200] Ibid. (emphasis in original).

[201] Ibid., 334.

allows Jesus to return to Nazareth, without the obligation just referred to forming any hindrance."[202]

The ambivalence theory also explains why the Virgin Mary and Joseph failed to understand the Boy Jesus' twin questions:

> A third reason to accept that εν τοις του πατρος μου is an ambivalent expression is that Luke immediately follows it with the incomprehension of Jesus' parents at their son's statement (50). This observation is a signal, by which Luke makes his readers aware that 49 has another and deeper meaning than the obvious one.[203]

This deeper meaning not only confused Mary and Joseph, but Saint Luke's readers as well continue to search the depth of meaning attached to this dynamic yet elusive phrase.

Satisfied with ambivalence as the intentional approach of the evangelist, Biblical scholars complete the shift from an "either-or" to a "both-and" interpretation of εν τοις του πατρος μου.

> It seems justified to conclude that Luke used an enigmatic turn of phrase with two meanings. The first, which in spite of its unusual wording impresses itself on the reader of the Greek text, is "I must be in the house of my Father, i.e. the temple". The second is "I must be about my Father's business".[204]

---

[202] Ibid.

[203] Ibid.

[204] Ibid., 335.

Although not strictly adhering to this ambivalence, Laurentin attaches a dual meaning to the mystifying phrase εν τοις του πατρος μου. According to one scholar, "Laurentin too attaches two meanings to the words εν τοις του πατρος μου: (1) 'with my Father in the temple': (2) 'with my Father in heaven after the resurrection and ascension.'"[205] This interpretation answers two contextual criticisms. First, the Boy Jesus would be free to return with His parents to Nazareth in obedience "because Jesus' words 'I must be with the Father' form a prophetic allusion to his resurrection and ascension. As this would not take place for another eighteen years, Jesus was not in conflict with his words in 49 when he returned to Nazareth: his hour had not yet come (John ii. 4)."[206] Second, Mary and Joseph's lack of understanding as to Jesus' first recorded words occurs because of His reference to His πατρος.[207] This confused the Boy Jesus' parents because they did not understand fully His intentional differentiation between His heavenly Father and His earthly father.

The ambivalence theory combines elements of both place and thing into the seemingly impenetrable phrase εν τοις του πατρος μου. In the next chapter, the integration theory goes a step further by incorporating all three forms of a noun – person, place, and thing – into the translation.

---

[205] Ibid., 334 fn 1.
[206] Ibid.
[207] Laurentin, *Jésus au Temple*, 72.

CHAPTER TWELVE

THEORY FIVE: INTEGRATION

> My sweetest Jesus! on Thy Mother's breast
> Thy little Face is radiant with love,
> Deign to reveal to me the mystery blest
> That draws Thee down to exile from above.
> Let me hide with Thee 'neath her veil of snow,
> That now conceals Thee from all human sight.
> Alone with Thee, bright Morning Star, I'll know
> On earth a foretaste of heaven's deep delight.[208]

The ambivalence theory included both place and thing into its formula. Another term for place is spatial; another term for thing is functional. In addition to these two aspects, one author adds person, referred to as personal, in seeking to combine all three aspects of a noun – person, place, and thing – into the Boy Jesus' first recorded words εν τοις του πατρος μου. "Apparently Luke 2:49 can be interpreted either in spatial, functional, or personal terms. But which is most correct? Or is an integrated interpretation of Luke 2:49, which would take these different dimensions of meaning all into account, possible?"[209] This chapter will address

---

[208] Sister Teresa of Lisieux, "The Dew Divine," 55.

[209] Weinert, "The Multiple Meanings of Luke 2:49 and Their Significance," 20.

these three aspects individually before seeking a possible integration.

First, Biblical scholars focus upon the spatial sense of the missing noun following εν τοις.

> Today, many scholars favor reading the phrase *en tois tou patros mou* with an emphasis on its spatial sense. In this vein, the favored translation is "in my Father's house" (in analogy to the French: *chez mon Pere*); the word "house" is added to the Greek text, with the implication that Jesus here is referring to the Temple.[210]

This reference to place appears to be the most commonly used.

Second, shifting from place, Biblical scholars focus on thing. "A second approach to the phrase *en tois tou patros mou* in Luke 2:49 is to interpret it functionally. Thus Jesus' saying is translated: 'Did you not know that I must be (involved) in my Father's affairs?' "[211] This relevant shift from where to what places more emphasis upon Jesus' activities within the temple rather than the temple itself.

Two critiques of this functional approach come to mind. "The difficulty here is that no exact parallels to the phrase in Luke 2:49 appear in other biblical texts. What is more, the functional translation tends to be rather abstract for this particular Lucan narrative context."[212] The context of the entire pericope focuses more on the concrete location

---

[210] Ibid., 19.

[211] Ibid., 20.

[212] Ibid.

of the event and the twelve-year-old Jesus speaking simply rather than with unnecessary complexity.

Besides place and thing, the phrase εν τοις του πατρος μου may articulate person. "From this standpoint, Jesus' saying would read: 'Did you not know that I must be among those (who belong to) my Father?' "[213] Similarly, "after three days, they found Him in the temple, sitting in the midst of the teachers, listening to them and asking them questions."[214] According to these scholars focusing on the personal, the Boy Jesus indicated His desire to be interacting with the temple teachers as they discussed the things of God.

According to the integration theory, all three aspects of a noun – person, place, and thing – find inclusion in the Boy Jesus' first recorded words. Under this theory, Saint Luke the evangelist intended to include personal, spatial, and functional elements into Jesus' response, and all three aspects bear serious consideration. "Such data from within the text, then whether it be Luke's use of prepositional phrases, his construction of Mary's question, or his wording of Jesus' reply, all suggest that Jesus himself understood 2:49 in personal and functional as well as spatial terms."[215] Such an integrated approach explains why scholars have debated this issue for centuries without reaching consensus. "Thus it is hardly surprising that interpreters of 2:49 repeatedly come up with one or more of these meanings in their work. The question remains, however, why commentators still seem compelled to choose one meaning over the others?"[216]

---

[213] Ibid.

[214] Luke 2:46 NASB.

[215] Weinert, "The Multiple Meanings of Luke 2:49 and Their Significance," 21.

[216] Ibid.

To answer this question, one scholar seeks to shift the direction of the debate. In this regard, the following question is posed: "And is there a way in which we can preserve the multifaceted meaning of this text and yet still grasp Luke's intent in 2:49 as a unity?"[217] The next chapter will describe such an attempt at unity under the pericope's overall emphasis on the Boy Jesus' pilgrimage to Jerusalem.

---

[217] Ibid.

CHAPTER THIRTEEN

THEORY SIX: PILGRIMAGE

Teach me, Father, how to go
Softly as the grasses grow;
Hush my soul to meet the shock
Of the wild world as a rock;
But my spirit, propt with power,
Make as simple as a flower.
Let the dry heart fill its cup,
Like a poppy looking up;
Let life lightly wear her crown,
Like a poppy looking down,
When its heart is filled with dew,
And its life begins anew.

Teach me, Father, how to be
Kind and patient as a tree.
Joyfully the crickets croon
Under shady oak at noon;
Beetle, on his mission bent,
Tarries in that cooling tent.
Let me, also, cheer a spot,
Hidden field or garden grot—
Place where passing souls can rest

On the way, and be their best.[218]

"It is interesting that one key motif in 2:41-50, which regularly seems to be overlooked almost as quickly as it is noticed, is the theme of pilgrimage."[219] The pilgrimage motif, present in the Lucan pericope, incorporates all three elements – person (personal), place (spatial), and thing (functional) – into its analysis.

Clearly, one embarking on a pilgrimage begins from an established place and seeks a distant destination. "As such, the dynamics of pilgrimage are profoundly spatial. In true pilgrimage, one regularly sets out from a familiar place (the place of assembly) and travels, by way of a specified route, to a far place (usually a sacred shrine)."[220] The journey shifts spatially, from one place to another.

Besides place, the pilgrimage theory focuses attention upon an array of activities. These activities achieve relevance within the journey itself. "Just as important is the power of pilgrimage to transform participants as they approach their goal, restoring in them a sense of wholeness, of salvation or, depending on one's viewpoint, of social 'fit' between expectation, experience, and duty."[221] Both the Boy Jesus' pilgrimage to Jerusalem and His interaction with the temple doctors combine to explain "why the interpretation stubbornly persists that the phrase *en tois tou patros mou*

---

[218] Edwin Markham, "A Prayer," quoted in *The Questing Spirit: Religion in the Literature of Our Time*, 400.

[219] Weinert, "The Multiple Meanings of Luke 2:49 and Their Significance," 21.

[220] Ibid.

[221] Ibid.

in Luke 2:49 refers to Jesus' involvement in his Father's activities/works/affairs."[222]

The spatial and functional aspects of pilgrimage are readily apparent. In addition, if we direct attention upon the pilgrims themselves, we discern a personal attribute essential to the pilgrimage experience.

> For one thing, it is widely understood that those who go on pilgrimage voluntarily assume a responsibility that goes beyond the normal limits of social and religious duty – a feature which makes pilgrims stand out from ordinary society. For another, the benefits of salvific transformation sought and achieved through pilgrimages generally are seen as accruing mainly to the individual pilgrim rather than to the group. This person-based, person-oriented, individuating and independent quality of the pilgrims' undertaking heightens what we today would call the "personal" dimension of their action.[223]

This personal aspect merges with the spatial and functional to provide an all-encompassing picture of the pilgrimage pericope.

"In short, within its present context of pilgrimage, Luke can use the saying in 2:49 simultaneously to affirm Jesus' unique place in God's saving plan, his active role therein, and the distinctly personal bond with God that this implies."[224] The spatial denotes the Boy Jesus' place in God's plan; the functional asserts Jesus' active role; and the per-

---

[222] Ibid., 21-22.
[223] Ibid., 22.
[224] Ibid.

sonal bond between Jesus and His heavenly Father is emphasized.

By including the spatial, functional, and personal aspects of this pericope into our analysis, Saint Luke directs his readers' attention upon the Boy Jesus. "In this story Jesus' extraordinary behavior, coupled with his parents' lack of comprehension, also helps Luke to transform his reader's view of Jesus."[225] As Jesus came to earth to transform humanity, so too a pilgrimage transforms the faithful pilgrim. "Through this changed perception Luke enables his readers to share something of the transforming power of the pilgrimage experience."[226]

"As a final note, the pilgrimage motif also suggests a way of translating Luke 2:49 more effectively into English."[227] Such a translation becomes necessary because current interpretations focusing on only one of the three aspects of a noun appear inadequate.

> Present translations, such as "Did you not know that I had to be in my Father's (house)?," or "…(involved) in my Father's (affairs)?," both suffer from the same defect. Both stress only one of the three senses of 2:49; and in both cases the personal force of Jesus' statement in 2:49 is muted.[228]

Based upon the pilgrimage, and seeking to incorporate the three possible singular interpretations into a comprehensive

---

[225] Ibid.
[226] Ibid.
[227] Ibid.
[228] Ibid.

unity, one scholar offers the following translation of εν τοις του πατρος μου.

> Taking the clue from Luke's reference to the *synodia* (or group of pilgrim fellow-travellers) in 2:44, I would propose to translate Luke 2:49 as: "Did you not know that I had to be in my Father's (company)?" This translation exploits the multiple meanings of the word "company," which in English can designate personal proximity, social gathering, or alliance in a joint enterprise. Thus the spatial, personal, and dynamic dimensions of Jesus' remark in 2:49 are preserved, without pressing the notion of God's "household" so far as to compromise Jesus' unique relationship to God.[229]

The integration of the spatial, functional, and personal elements of possible interpretations is complete.

Despite this positive possibility, the pilgrimage theory, though quite thorough in its analysis and comprehensive in its scope, still falls short of complete certainty. As the Virgin Mary and Saint Joseph enter the temple, and Mary questions her Son and shares her concern, it's hard to imagine a twelve-year-old boy responding to His mother's simple inquiry with such a complex and multifaceted response. The pilgrimage theory therefore may fall short by neglecting the Boy Jesus' innocence and youth, inserting unnecessary complexity to a response calling for stark simplicity.

....

[229] Ibid.

CHAPTER FOURTEEN

THE BOY JESUS IN THE TEMPLE

O Jesus, little brother dear!
   For us from Heaven didst Thou flee;
Thou knowest well Thy bird-cage here
   Is Carmel, and Thy birds are we.

The little bird it always sings,
   Nor fear for its small meal doth know;
A grain of wheat contentment brings;
   It sows not, spins not, here below.
Within this cage where we have fled,
   Is all provided through Thy care;
The one thing needful, Thou hast said,
   Is just to love Thee, Child most fair!
So, through the hours, we sing Thy praise,
   With glad, pure spirits ever blest.
We know the angels, all the days,
   Love Carmel's birds within their nest.

Jesu! Thy bitter tears to dry,
   That sinful men have wrung from Thee,
Thy birds to win back souls will try,
   By their sweet songs of ecstasy.
One day, when earth and time are o'er,

> And Thy clear call to us is given,
> Then angel-hands shall open the door;
> Thy birds shall take their flight to Heaven;
> And there, with charming, songful hosts
> Of little cherubs glad and gay,
> Thy happy birds from Carmel's coasts
> Shall praise Thy Holy Name alway.[230]

Jesus was a twelve-year-old Jewish boy visiting Jerusalem for the Passover celebration, possibly for the first time in His life. Raised in Nazareth by the Virgin Mary and Joseph as a simple carpenter's son, the Boy Jesus still would have been immersed in the study of Sacred Scripture both at home and within the local synagogue. Actually being able to visit the temple in Jerusalem and to listen to and speak with the doctors and teachers of the Law undoubtedly would have been one of the most exciting events in the young boy's life. These teachers would not have been impressed by nuanced statements they could not understand. Rather, Jesus' clear and precise insights into God's Word, in congruence with a humble and listening heart, would have touched the temple teachers.

"Jesus learned as other children learned. His advancement in learning may have been more rapid than that of other children since there was no sin in His life to retard that learning. But He did go through a process of learning."[231] In this regard, like other children, Jesus benefitted from a variety of sources.

---

[230] Sister Teresa of Lisieux, "The Bird Cage of the Infant Jesus," 116-117.

[231] Colton, *Expository Studies in the Life of Christ*, 58.

There was a mental growth, because He was "filled with wisdom." Wisdom is not mere information, nor talents. It is something more of the heart than of the intellect, containing earnestness and love. It ponders life, seeking to understand its mystery and purpose. Jesus had helps to this end, such as Mary, His mother, the Holy Scriptures, and the sacred book of nature, as means to develop His mind.[232]

The Boy Jesus visits the temple with a hungry heart willing to listen and learn.

"As God, in Him were all the treasures of wisdom and knowledge. But as a child He was not endowed with infinite knowledge, his mind being alert, eager to gain knowledge and attain to wisdom."[233] The Boy Jesus learned like all other children, not fully grasping lessons at first sight, but studying and retaining information by trial and error. "There is a deep significance in the fact Jesus was once a child with child's thoughts, feelings of joy, griefs and trials."[234] At some point in time, "the soul of the boy awoke to see and know God as he is known only to pure and loving hearts."[235]

The Boy Jesus' visit to the temple reveals this pattern of learning as Jesus sat "in the midst of the teachers, both listening to them and asking them questions."[236] One can imagine the temple scene and understand why the teachers were so eager to converse with the Boy Jesus.

[232] Anderson, *Gospel Firsts: Messages on the First Things in the Bible*, 45.

[233] Ibid.

[234] Idid., 48-49.

[235] Landrum, "Consecrated Childhood," 213.

[236] Luke 2:46b NASB.

It is observed – so far as inquiry is able to look back at this distance in time – that at his being a schoolboy he was an early questionist, quietly inquisitive, "why this was, and that was not, to be remembered? Why this was granted, and that denied?" This being mixed with a remarkable modesty, and a sweet serene quietness of nature, and with them a quick apprehension of many perplexed parts of learning, imposed then on him as a scholar, made his master and others to believe him to have an inward, blessed, Divine light, and therefore to consider him to be a little wonder.[237]

It becomes clear "Jesus, though He had knowledge far beyond the expectation for a child of His age, continued to seek more knowledge by asking questions."[238]

The epicenter and essence of this temple visit occurs when Jesus, for the first time in any Gospel account, publicly proclaims His familial understanding of God as His heavenly Father. "The center of the story is not the boy's intelligence but his reference to God as his Father in vs. 49. This is highly Christological, for here we have Jesus saying of himself what the heavenly voice will say at the baptism."[239] "Now when all the people were baptized, it came to pass, that Jesus also being baptized, and praying, the heaven was opened, And the Holy Ghost descended in a bodily shape like a dove upon him, and a voice came from heaven, which said, Thou art my beloved Son; in thee I am well pleased."[240]

---

[237] Hastings, *The Great Texts of the Bible: St. Luke*, 118.

[238] Colton, *Expository Studies in the Life of Christ*, 64.

[239] Brown, *The Birth of the Messiah*, 483.

[240] Luke 3:21-22 KJV.

Although we cannot grasp this divine mystery with any degree of certainty, perhaps at the age of twelve in the temple, the Boy Jesus understood His unique relationship to God at its deepest, most intimate level to date.

> But it was the opening of his human faculties, the quickening of their activities, to grasp the objects which were to fill and enlist his powers, which marked the commencement of that higher consciousness and ampler realization of the truth, in meek and zealous obedience to which he from that time forward went forth, and which was the active principle of all his subsequent life and deeds as the Redeemer of the world.[241]

The eternal necessity expressed by the use of the Greek word δει in Luke 2:49 is repeated often in this and the other Gospels.

> A similar sense of obligation appears in subsequent Lucan passages precisely when Jesus is speaking of the role the Father has given him to play. "I must preach the good news of the kingdom of God to other cities also, for I was sent for this purpose" (4:43). "The Son of Man must suffer many things ... be killed ... and on the third day be raised" (9:22; see also 17:25; 22:37; 24:7,26). "Behold I cast out demons and perform cures today and tomorrow, and the third day I must finish my course; nevertheless, I must go on my way today, tomorrow, and the day following" (13:32-33).[242]

---

[241] Seiss, *Lectures on the Gospels*, 199.

[242] Brown, *The Birth of the Messiah*, 491.

The Boy Jesus nurtured these imperatives in His heart. "Such was Jesus when twelve years old. In his soul there was a vivid consciousness of God, his nearness and his fatherhood. That consciousness seemed to prophesy the possibility of an unusual life and a religious mission."[243]

Although it cannot be proven with any degree of certainty, perhaps Jesus during this pivotal temple visit fully understood both God as His heavenly Father and His own ultimate redemptive mission. "But even at the age of twelve He knew that there was a special mission on which He had been sent and it was the passion of His soul to fulfill that mission."[244] Beginning at some moment in time during His early years, perhaps this one, Jesus "was under a constant and ever-increasing obligation to carry his work through to the end. He did nothing without the sense of 'oughtness' being upon Him."[245] The resulting self-realization caused by becoming aware of only one of these truths would be overwhelming. If the Boy Jesus both understood God as His Father and comprehended His divine mission during this temple visit, this event might be the most significant occurrence during the first thirty years of His earthly existence. Imagine the Boy Jesus trying to express Himself by putting into words his dual life-changing awareness when He first sees the two people, the Blessed Virgin Mary and Saint Joseph, dearest to His heart!

What precise meaning did the Boy Jesus intend to share when uttering the phrase εν τοις του πατρος μου? These are the words of a twelve-year-old boy, filled with a deep

---

[243] Barton, *Jesus of Nazareth*, 97.
[244] Colton, *Expository Studies in the Life of Christ*, 68-69.
[245] Pentecost, *The Birth and Boyhood of Jesus*, 394.

and abiding love for His heavenly Father, striving mightily to communicate to those closest to Him on earth. Saint Luke undoubtedly had numerous first-hand recollections from Mary and other people who knew Jesus during the first thirty years of His life. Wonderfully, in penning the Boy Jesus' first recorded words, the evangelist leaves us with an ambiguous phrase – εν τοις του πατρος μου – offering an unlimited array of legitimate possibilities drawing the reader closer and closer to the truth.

EPILOGUE

BEST FRIENDS FOREVER

Dear Jesus! 'tis Thy Holy Face
  Is here the star that guides my way;
Thy countenance, so full of grace,
  Is heaven on earth, to me, to-day;
And love finds holy charms for me
  In Thy sweet eyes with tear-drops wet;
Through mine own tears I smile at Thee,
  And in Thy griefs my pains forget.

How gladly would I live unknown,
  Thus to console Thy aching heart!
Thy veiled beauty, it is shown
  To those who live from earth apart.
I long to fly to Thee alone!

Thy Face is now my fatherland,—
  The radiant sunshine of my days,—
My realm of love, my sunlit land,
  Where, all life long, I sing Thy praise;
It is the lily of the vale,
  Whose mystic perfume, freely given,
Brings comfort, when I faint and fail,
  And makes me taste the peace of heaven.

> Thy Face, in its unearthly grace,
>   Is like divinest myrrh to me,
> That on my heart I gladly place;
>   It is my lyre of melody;
> My rest — my comfort — is Thy Face.
>
> My only wealth, Lord! is thy Face;
>   I ask naught else than this from Thee;
> Hid in the secret of that Face,
>   The more I shall resemble Thee!
> Oh, leave on me some impress faint
>   Of Thy sweet, humble, patient Face,
> And soon I shall become a saint,
>   And draw men to Thy saving grace.
>
> So, in the secret of Thy Face,
>   Oh! hide me, hide me, Jesus blest!
> There let me find its hidden grace,
>   Its holy fires, and, in heaven's rest,
> Its rapturous kiss, in Thy embrace![246]

Jesus and Mary are our best friends forever. Imagine Saint Luke travelling to speak with the Blessed Virgin Mary about what it was like to give birth to Jesus, nurse Him from her breasts, share in His enthusiastic joy and laughter, and console him when His heart hurt or His flesh bled and He cried. With much laughter and some tears, the Blessed Virgin Mary may have brought to life some amazing memories about what it meant to be the Mother of God, the Mother of the Boy Jesus.

---

[246] Sister Teresa of Lisieux, "Canticle to the Holy Face," 7.

Saint Luke left the Virgin Mary and travelled back home with much to consider. What a special privilege and blessing this audience must have been for him, to share in these precious memories of Our Lady. Upon returning home, he may have knelt in prayer to thank his heavenly Father because of his deepening love for the Boy Jesus and for the fact that with these childhood memories, "His mother treasured all these things in her heart."[247] As Saint Luke continued to pray for the inspiration of the Holy Spirit in the writing of his Gospel account, he decided to write detailed descriptions about the Annunciation and the Angel Gabriel, the Visitation with Elizabeth, the Birth of Jesus in a cave, and the Presentation of the Baby Jesus in the temple.

Perhaps Saint Luke continued on his knees in prayer. Overwhelmed with the powerful and poignant memories of the Blessed Virgin Mary, Saint Luke may have prayed furiously for one more bit of inspiration, one single event and interaction from the first three decades of the life of Jesus, one historical occurrence with divine implications expressing the joyful sorrow in the lives of Jesus and Mary. Inspired by the Holy Ghost, he finally decides upon the Finding of the Boy Jesus in the Temple. Perhaps for Saint Luke the evangelist, following this most special and inspirational prayer, Jesus and Mary became his best friends forever.

Ultimately, the Lucan pericope of the Boy Jesus in the temple is not concerned primarily with the precise meaning of εν τοις του πατρος μου. Although Biblical scholars have debated this interpretive issue for centuries, it is at best only of lesser concern. Though relevant, as all Scripture is rele-

---

[247] Luke 2:51b NASB.

vant, the precise interpretation of these five Greek words is tertiary to the two truths revealed by this story.

Primarily, for the first time in any Gospel account, Jesus acknowledges God as His heavenly Father. "This statement seems to indicate that Jesus had already developed the habit of thinking on the things of the Heavenly Father. He had, no doubt, considered His relationship with the Heavenly Father many times before this incident, but here we have His public declaration of it."[248] Secondarily, the Boy Jesus understood and accepted God's unique call on His life, His mission of redemption, at this very early age. "Here is a public expression of His wholehearted dedication to the will of His Heavenly Father. He never lost sight of this objective. It was before Him night and day. Frequently He made reference to this supreme passion of His soul to do the will of His Heavenly Father and to finish His work."[249]

For all the scholarship written upon it throughout the centuries, the precise meaning of εν τοις του πατρος μου involves only one part of a much larger story.

> In any case, the first words attributed to Jesus in the Lucan Gospel form a statement about his relationship to his heavenly Father. What is significant is that it is uttered by him somewhere in the Jerusalem Temple. This is true, no matter what interpretation is given to *en tois tou patros mou* – for the sense of the relationship comes through no matter which interpretation of these words is used.[250]

---

[248] Colton, *Expository Studies in the Life of Christ*, 67.
[249] Ibid., 69.
[250] Fitzmyer, "The Gospel According to Luke (I-IX)," 437.

This intimate relationship between Father and Son "was the deep secret of all His wonderful life."[251] "Our sounding-lines are not long enough to touch bottom in this great word from the lips of a boy of twelve; but this is clear, that as He grew into self-consciousness, there came with it the growing consciousness of His Sonship to His Father in heaven. In these words we find that Christ is both conscious of, and lays claim to His Sonship with the Father."[252] To perceive God as Father necessitates one's own self-awareness as being God's special Son. This inevitably leads to a deeper understanding of Jesus' earthly surroundings, with every aspect of life sublimated and serving this most intimate and divine Father-Son relationship. "We have only to note that the Child Jesus, at the age of twelve years, certainly knew He was the Son of God, and that henceforth all His relations and life must be regulated by that great fact."[253]

Recognizing this divine and eternal familial relationship, the Boy Jesus discovered His purpose in life. "Every life which has any value or any force finds a ruling principle or purpose which steadily guides it."[254] Jesus left the temple knowing God as Father and Himself as called to a unique mission. "When only twelve Jesus had grasped the great idea that life must be lived for a purpose."[255] Jesus' primary purpose involved doing His Father's will. Regardless of whether one supplies the term "house" or "business" or "things" into Luke 2:49, Jesus reminds His parents that He must be about

---

[251] Pentecost, *The Birth and Boyhood of Jesus*, 376.
[252] Maclaren, *After the Resurrection*, 195-196.
[253] Pentecost, *The Birth and Boyhood of Jesus*, 381.
[254] Hastings, *The Great Texts of the Bible: St. Luke*, 113.
[255] Ibid., 134.

His Father's unique call on His life. "As in a mountain lake one sees reflected the mountains and the forests and the procession of the clouds, so in this single sentence of Jesus is mirrored the entire New Testament land and sky."[256]

The Boy Jesus answered His Father's call for the rest of His earthly existence. "But the real authority in his life is his heavenly Father; and his life's work will lead him back to the Temple again, where he will claim his own authority, and where this time the religious leaders will conspire to kill him."[257] Intimacy with His heavenly Father led ultimately to the Cross.

> Responsibility, then, answerable to another for His life and His use of it, but that other His Heavenly Father, whom it was the joy of His loving heart to serve – there is the principle and purpose which we find at the heart of Him at twelve years old; it will go with Him through life. It will be there still when with dying lips He will cry, "It is finished!" – finished, the work God gave Him to do; "Father, into thy hands I commend my spirit."[258]

Our lifelong friendship with Jesus Christ begins at His birth with the Blessed Virgin Mary, continues during His childhood as we meet Him and His Mother in the temple, and culminates as we faithfully stand with Our Lady at the foot of the Cross.

---

[256] Ibid., 127.

[257] Chakoian, "Luke 2:41-52," 190.

[258] Hastings, *The Great Texts of the Bible: St. Luke*, 114.

"The best time in life to find and know God through His Son Jesus is the time of childhood."[259] The Boy Jesus mirrored this intimacy for us in His historic visit to the Jerusalem temple at the age of twelve.

> See how great a love the Father has bestowed on us, that we would be called children of God; and such we are. Or this reason the world does not know us, because it did not know Him. Beloved, now we are children of God, and it has not appeared as yet what we will be. We know that when He appears, we will be like Him, because we will see Him just as He is. And everyone who has this hope fixed on Him purifies himself, just as He is pure.[260]

To the extent we befriend the Boy Jesus and walk in His footprints, we love both His heavenly Father and His Virgin Mother.

Our emerging friendship with Jesus nurtures our love of His Father. Jesus' "whole attitude of life gave voice to this inner consciousness of divine relationship. His every utterance concerning God expressed this deep seated, abiding and unshakable conviction of his sonship. All the activities of his life were interpreted by this relationship."[261] As Saint Paul writes, we too can claim this sonship:

> But when the fullness of the time came, God sent forth His Son, born of a woman, born under the Law, so that He might redeem those who were under the Law, that

---

[259] Colton, *Expository Studies in the Life of Christ*, 67.

[260] 1 John 3:1-3 NASB.

[261] J. C. Massie, *The Ten Greatest Sayings of Jesus* (New York: Doran, 1927), 17.

we might receive the adoption as sons. Because you are sons, God has sent forth the Spirit of His Son into our hearts, crying, "Abba! Father!" Therefore you are no longer a slave, but a son; and if a son, then an heir through God."[262]

The English poet William Wordsworth beautifully describes the life cycle from birth through boyhood, youth, and adulthood to death:

> Our birth is but a sleep and a forgetting:
> The Soul that rises with us, our life's Star,
>   Hath had elsewhere its setting,
>   And cometh from afar;
>   Not in entire forgetfulness,
>   And not in utter nakedness,
> But trailing clouds of glory do we come
> From God, who is our home;
> Heaven lies about us in our infancy!
> Shades of the prison-house begin to close
>   Upon the growing Boy,
> But he beholds the light, and whence it flows,
>   He sees it in his joy;
> The Youth, who daily farther from the east
>   Must travel, still is Nature's Priest,
>   And by the vision splendid
>   Is on his way attended;
> At length the Man perceives it die away,
> And fade into the light of common day. [263]

---

[262] Galatians 4:4-7 NASB.

[263] Massie, *The Ten Greatest Sayings of Jesus*, 17.

Although we find our home in God, our spiritual eyes may go dim with age. The growing boy "beholds the light"; the youth "still is Nature's Priest"; yet the man loses sight of heaven as he watches the light "fade into the light of common day."[264]

Jesus' transition from boyhood to manhood took an opposite course:

> By stressing Mary's retention of the things that happened, puzzling to understand their meaning, Luke is giving us a perceptive theological insight into history: there was a continuity from the infant Jesus to the boy Jesus to the Jesus of the ministry to the risen Jesus; and when Christian disciples like Mary believed in Jesus as God's Son after the resurrection, they were finding adequate expression for intuitions that had begun long ago.[265]

The Blessed Virgin Mary showed us the way and continues to guide our steps towards Jesus. Imagine the young teenage girl hearing this message from the Angel Gabriel: "The Holy Ghost shall come upon thee, and the power of the Highest shall overshadow thee: therefore also that holy thing which shall be born of thee shall be called the Son of God."[266] Mary believed and spoke in humble submission, "Behold the handmaid of the Lord; be it unto me according to thy word."[267] From that moment in her young life, the

---

[264] Ibid.

[265] Brown, *The Birth of the Messiah*, 494.

[266] Luke 1:35 KJV.

[267] Ibid., Luke 1:38a.

Blessed Virgin Mary loved God like no one ever before or since, and Jesus began His human life in her womb. From the womb to the tomb, Mary was there, and her friendship brings us closer to both her Son and His heavenly Father.

By the age of twelve, Jesus with His first recorded words understood and expressed His unique divine Sonship to His heavenly Father. With our best friends Jesus as our Brother and Mary as our Mother, we too become sons and heirs of our heavenly Father. Like the Boy Jesus, we are called to an intimate relationship with God: "Shall not a child love to speak with his Father, and hear his Father speak to him? It must be so; it will be so; it cannot help being so with you if you feel the child-spirit strong within you as our blessed Lord and Master did when but twelve years of age."[268] Like the Virgin Mary, we are called to see beyond the mundane into the divine:

> To see a World in a grain of sand,
> And a Heaven in a wild flower,
> Hold Infinity in the palm of your hand,
> And Eternity in an hour.[269]

As Orthodox believers, our special friendship with Jesus and Mary brings us into a familial relationship with God the Father. Like the Boy Jesus in the temple, we are called to an intimacy with God far more than we could ever ask or imagine. This communion began the moment we were

---

[268] Spurgeon, *C.H. Spurgeon's Sermons on Crises in the Life of Jesus*, 16.

[269] William Blake, "Auguries of Innocence," *The Poetical Works of William Blake*, ed. John Sampson (London: Oxford University, 1934), 171.

immersed in the baptismal waters and sealed with the chrism oil. "Such a moment is never forgotten, the moment at which the boy ceases to see through the eyes of others, ceases to speak, to think, as others do about him; when he sees with his own eyes, and faces his own world, and seeks for his own interpretation of it."[270] Like the Virgin Mary in the temple, we are called to seek Jesus with all our hearts and to protect our love for Him with all our might. We need to be willing to stand in sorrow with Our Lady at the foot of the Cross.

"'Believe me,' he said, 'unless you change your whole outlook and become like little children you will never enter the Kingdom of Heaven.'"[271] Like the Boy Jesus nurtured by the Blessed Virgin Mary, we are called to see life with the childlike eyes of faith.

> Jesus saw things just as his Father saw them in his creative imagination, when willing them out to the eyes of his children. But if he could always see the things of his Father even as some men and more children see them at times, he might well feel almost at home among them. He could not cease to admire, cease to love them. I say love, because the life in them, the presence of the creative One, would ever be plain to him. In the Perfect would familiarity ever destroy wonder at things essentially wonderful because essentially divine?[272]

---

[270] Hastings, *The Great Texts of the Bible: St. Luke*, 126.
[271] J. B. Phillips, *The Gospels* (New York: Macmillan, 1953), 38.
[272] MacDonald, *The Hope of the Gospel*, 56-58.

As a child of God in love with our best friends Jesus and Mary, we too are called to live in wonder, praying on our knees before our heavenly Father, immersing ourselves in the sanctity and sacraments of the Orthodox Church, studying the truth of the Bible, loving our neighbor as ourselves, and even loving our enemies.

"For now we see in a mirror dimly, but then face to face. Now I know in part, but then I will know fully, just as I also have been fully known."[273] We are called to look with the eyes of faith, to see like a child, to take the Virgin Mary's hand and walk in the footprints of the Boy Jesus. " 'And now here is my secret, a very simple secret: It is only with the heart that one can see rightly; what is essential is invisible to the eye.' "[274] Seeing with the eyes of faith, the Boy Jesus both understood His Sonship and accepted His Father's eternal mission. After Mary and Joseph found Jesus in the temple, "he went down with them and came to Nazareth, and was obedient to them."[275] The Virgin Mary chose humility in loving the Son of God while the Boy Jesus chose obedience to the Mother of God.

"The child sees things as the Father means him to see them, as he thought of them when he uttered them. For God is not only the Father of the child, but of the childhood that constitutes him a child, therefore the childness is of the divine nature."[276] Like the Boy Jesus and the Virgin Mary, we too are called to embrace the wonder of salvation as children of God called to an eternal purpose.

---

[273] 1 Corinthians 13:12 NASB.

[274] Antoine de Saint-Exupéry, *The Little Prince* (San Diego: Harcourt Brace, 1971), 73.

[275] Luke 2:51a NRSV.

[276] MacDonald, *The Hope of the Gospel*, 57.

Two thousand years ago, Jesus and Mary, our best friends forever, showed us the Way.

BIBLIOGRAPHY

Anderson, David E. *Gospel Firsts: Messages on the First Things in the Bible.* N.p.: Anderson, 1947.

Baer, Dallas C. *The Old Gospel for the New Times*, vol. 1. Burlington, VT: Lutheran Literary Board, 1936.

Barton, George A. *Jesus of Nazareth.* New York: Macmillan, 1932.

Bible or Not, "It is Always Darkest Before the Dawn," accessed October 4, 2010, http://bibleornot.org/its-it-is-always-darkest-before-the-dawn/.

Blake, William. "Auguries of Innocence," *The Poetical Works of William Blake*, ed. John Sampson. London: Oxford University, 1934.

Brown, Raymond E. *The Birth of the Messiah.* New York: Doubleday, 1993.

Chakoian, Karen. "Luke 2:41-52." *Interpretation* 52 (1998): 185-190.

Chrysostom, Saint. "Homilies on the Gospel of St. John." *A Select Library of the Nicene and Post-Nicene Fathers of the Christian Church*, ed. Philip Schaff, vol. XIV. Edinburgh: T&T Clark, 1989.

Colton, C. E. *Expository Studies in the Life of Christ*. Grand Rapids, MI: Zondervan, 1957.

Deiss, Lucien. *Joseph, Mary, Jesus*, trans. Madeleine Beaumont. Collegeville, MN: Liturgical Press, 1996.

Dyke, Henry van. *The Lost Boy*. New York: Harper, 1914.

Fitzmyer, Joseph A. "The Gospel According to Luke (I-IX)." *The Anchor Bible* Garden City, NY: Doubleday, 1981.

Francis of Assisi, Saint. *Francis and Clare: The Complete Works*, trans. Regis J. Armstrong and Ignatius C. Brady. New York: Paulist Press, 1982.

Garvie, Alfred E. *Studies in the Inner Life of Jesus*. New York: Hodder & Stoughton, 1907.

Hastings, James, ed. *The Great Texts of the Bible: St. Luke*. Grand Rapids, MI: Baker, 1976.

Hawkins, John C. *Horae Synopticae: Contributions to the Study of the Synoptic Problem*, 2d ed. Oxford: Clarendon, 1909.

Hopkins, Gerard Manley. *Poems of Gerard Manley Hopkins*, 3rd ed., edited by W. H. Gardner. New York & London: Oxford University Press, 1948.

Jonge, Henk J. de. "Sonship, Wisdom, Infancy: Luke ii. 41-51a." *New Testament Studies* 24 (1978): 317-354.

Kendrick, A. C. *The Moral Conflict of Humanity and Other Papers*. Philadelphia: American Baptist PS, 1894.

Kilgallen, John J. "Luke 2, 41-50: Foreshadowing of Jesus, Teacher." *Biblica* 66 (1985): 553-559.

Landrum, William Warren. "Consecrated Childhood." *The American Baptist Pulpit at the Beginning of the Twentieth Century*, ed. Henry Thompson Louthan. Williamsburg, VA: n.n., 1903.

Laurentin, René. *Jésus au Temple*. Paris: Gabalda, 1966.

_____. *Structure et Théologie de Luc I – II*. Paris: Gabalda, 1957.

The Life of the Virgin, the Theotokos. Buena Vista, CA: Holy Apostles Convent, 1989.

Luccock, Halford E. and Frances Brentano, ed. *The Questing Spirit: Religion in the Literature of Our Time*. New York: Coward-McCann, 1947.

Maclaren, Alexander. *After the Resurrection*. New York: Funk & Wagnalls, n.d.

Manson, William. "The Gospel of Luke." *The Moffat New Testament Commentary*. New York: Hodder & Stoughton, 1963.

Massie, J. C. *The Ten Greatest Sayings of Jesus*. New York: Doran, 1927.

Maximus the Confessor. *The Life of the Virgin*, trans. Stephen J. Shoemaker. New Haven and London: Yale University Press, 2012.

Pentecost, George F. *The Birth and Boyhood of Jesus*. New York: ATS, 1897.

Phillips, J. B. *The Gospels*. New York: Macmillan, 1953.

Prat, Ferdinand. *Jesus Christ: His Life, His Teaching, and His Work*, trans. John J. Heenan, vol. 1. Milwaukee, WI: Bruce, 1950.

Saint-Exupéry, Antoine de. *The Little Prince*. San Diego: Harcourt Brace, 1971.

Seiss, Joseph A. *Lectures on the Gospels*, 4th ed. Philadelphia: General Council PH, 1908.

Spurgeon, C.H. *C.H. Spurgeon's Sermons on Crises in the Life of Jesus*, ed. Charles T. Cook, vol. 24. London: Marshall, 1966.

Temple, Patrick J. "What is to be understood by *En Tois* Luke 2, 49?" *The Irish Theological Quarterly* 17 (1922): 248-263.

Teresa of Lisieux, Sister. *The Petals of a "Little Flower"*, trans. Susan L. Emery. Boston: Angel Guardian Press, 1907.

Weinert, Francis D. "The Multiple Meanings of Luke 2:49 and Their Significance." *Biblical Theology Bulletin* 13 (1983): 19-22.

Whyte, Alexander. *The Walk, Conversation and Character of Jesus Christ our Lord*. Edinburgh: Oliphant, Anderson & Ferrier, 1905.

Wordsworth, William. "My Heart Leaps Up When I Behold." *Selected Poems of William Wordsworth*, ed. Solomon Francis Gingerich. Boston: Houghton Mifflin, 1923.

ABOUT THE AUTHOR

Deacon David Lochbihler, J.D., serves at the Holy Altar at Saint Patrick Orthodox Church and teaches Fourth Grade at The Fairfax Christian School in Virginia. After graduating *summa cum laude* from the University of Notre Dame and *cum laude* from the University of Texas School of Law, Deacon David worked as a Chicago attorney for three years before becoming a teacher and coach for three decades. He also earned three Master's degrees in Elementary Education, Biblical Studies, and Orthodox Theology. His varsity high school basketball and soccer teams captured four N.V.I.A.C. conference championships. He authored *Prayers to Our Lady East and West* (2021) and *The Joy of Orthodoxy* (2022).

PRAYERS
TO OUR LADY
EAST AND WEST

DEACON DAVID LOCHBIHLER, J.D.

ORTHODOX LOGOS PUBLISHING

THE JOY OF ORTHODOXY

DEACON DAVID LOCHBIHLER, J.D.

ORTHODOX LOGOS PUBLISHING

WWW.ORTHODOXLOGOS.COM

www.ingramcontent.com/pod-product-compliance
Lightning Source LLC
Chambersburg PA
CBHW042127100526
44587CB00026B/4204